THE

The New
COMMUNITY
IN CHRIST

Essays on the Corporate Christian Life

Edited by
JAMES H. BURTNESS
AND JOHN P. KILDAHL

AUGSBURG PUBLISHING HOUSE
Minneapolis 15, Minnesota

THE NEW COMMUNITY IN CHRIST

Scripture quotations are from the Revised Standard Version of the Bible, copyright 1946 and 1952 by the Division of Christian Education of the National Council of Churches.

Chapter III, "Unity and Diversity in the New Testament," is reprinted from *Student World*, Vol. LV, No. 1, First Quarter 1962. Chapter VI, "The Concept of Selfhood in the New Testament and Modern Ethics," is reprinted from *Religion and Life*, copyright © 1960 by Abingdon Press.

Manufactured in the United States of America

Foreword

To be a disciple of Jesus Christ is at once a highly solitary expedition and a fiercely corporate one. We are in him, and in him we are related to all who are in him as cells are related in a body. We are the church. But in Christ we have a more comprehensive company still: we return to all men, believers and unbelievers, as responsible brothers. I cannot have Christ alone by myself in some corner; I cannot even have him in cozy company with other disciples. He died for all men, and I live with him most fully when in love I reach out (as he reaches out) to all.

This volume speaks to me as a solitary person before God and it speaks to me as one of a great company. Each essay is as a spoke in a wheel converging at the hub in a central concern and theme.

There are six observations which have emerged for me in the reading of these essays.

First, the nine contributors are comparatively young men, all but one trained in the formal theological disciplines. While they are all working primarily within the Lutheran Church, each tries to speak to and for the whole of Christendom. The essays are not directed toward sharpening the particularities of the Lutheran tradition over against the rest of Christendom, but toward the problems and the objectives that involve all churches that confess Jesus Christ as

Lord and Savior. It is commendable that, as young men, they seek to give expression to the insights which their years have given. Twenty years later, were they to join again in a common effort, their perspectives may have changed (if not changed, deepened and broadened), but this does not diminish the significance of their contributions now.

Second, as the title indicates, the essayists, each within his own orbit, seek to clarify the significance of the church as a people apart, a people captured by God and belonging to God. This century, following hard upon the nineteenth with its surge of world mission activity, has forced the churches to confront one another and to ask the simple but complex question, "What are we?" "What is the Church?" One cannot ask this question without becoming involved in the place of the person and work of Jesus Christ, the significance of the prophets' and apostles' and evangelists' witness in the Holy Scriptures, the work of the Holy Spirit. The whole gamut of theological concerns is drawn into the discussion.

Third, if the church as the *New Community* is to have a reality other than an ideology, it is impossible to avoid the use of psychological and sociological categories. The temptation so to analyze the phenomenon of the *New Community* that it reflects no more than patterns of organization and behavior common to all corporate confluences of men is faced with candor and discernment. There is in this book a stalwart attempt to show that the *Community* is indeed a peculiar people.

Fourth, the highly individualistic aspect of discipleship, expressed in the I-thou encounter between God and man and issuing in a mystical or pietistic individualism, is dealt with in seriousness and sympathy. Is the individual (the believer) before or after the *Community* (the church)? Which comes first? The essayists face the suspicion that lurks in the minds of many outside of the *Community* that the church is but another sociological plot to obliterate the individual and swallow him up into some unambiguous, uniform mass. Only as men are captured by Christ and in Christ are compelled to accept one another freely and responsibly as brothers can they become truly human and escape the plight of the mass-man. The life in God through Jesus Christ by the power of the Holy Spirit is the key to community.

Fifth, the reader will find much help in the question of diversity and unity. Within the Christian family there is always the fear that diversity is the enemy of unity, and that only by some external device such as common propositions agreed upon or a uniform manner of life rigidly followed can unity safeguard itself from the rich diversity which seems constantly to threaten the *Community*. The reader will discover in these essays that which will allay these fears and, without abandoning the Lord's concern that we be one, accept diversity as one of the Lord's rich gifts to his Community.

Sixth, both as an individual follower of Christ and as a cell or member in the whole company of followers, I find the writers driving me relentlessly in three directions: (1) to God and his means of grace for the life itself, (2) to my fellow believers in this present age and back into the long corporate history of the heritage of the one, holy church, and (3) out into this world which we call "secular" but which is nonetheless the world for which Christ died and which defines the mission orbit of the church.

A. N. Rogness

Preface

These essays constitute an effort by a group of younger theologians to express some primary concerns about the interpretation of the Christian faith and life. A group was convened representing a variety of theological disciplines, and no specific direction was given for the essays except that they were to be based on honest research yet written for popular consumption. Each author was free to work out his essay in his own way. The happy thing that developed is that when the essays came in, it was clear that there was a sharper focal point to our concerns than we had imagined. Running through the various contributions is a common emphasis on the communal aspects of the Christian life.

Each man had been nurtured in that rugged but individualistic piety characteristic of the early part of this century. There is a distinct gratitude for this heritage. Yet the discovery of the reality of the church and the realization that one was actually a member of the very Body of Christ brought forth an overwhelming joy which spilled over into every area of life. It was clear that each writer was convinced that a purely individualistic interpretation of Christianity was neither true to the New Testament nor adequate for the living of the new life in Christ. Thus the title emerged: *The New Community in Christ.*

There is a great deal of diversity evident in this volume.

There are articles written by men whose major field of interest is New Testament, systematic theology, history of dogma, social ethics, clinical psychology, and even architecture. There are varieties of style and different emphases in content. Some are obviously written for a more specialized audience than others. But we believe that the reader will agree with us that, diverse as they are, they all are serious attempts to explore the implications of the corporate Christian life.

We are thankful to Dr. Alvin N. Rogness, president of Luther Theological Seminary, for kindly consenting to write the foreword, and to the Rev. William Gentz, book editor of Augsburg Publishing House, for his patient encouragement in this project.

JAMES H. BURTNESS
JOHN P. KILDAHL

Contents

9

I

The Corporate Character of the New Life

JOSEPH M. SHAW

"Close-Knit Congregation Puts Emphasis on the Individual," reads the headline of a newspaper article reporting the strong points of a certain local church group. In the body of the article one of the congregation's leaders is quoted as saying: "The Church revolves around you, the individual."[1]

Most Protestant church members, it is safe to say, would quickly and gladly endorse such publicity for their own congregations. And well they might, for no Protestant even faintly aware of the meaning of the Reformation would give his support to a form of church life which in any way appeared to be slighting the individual in promoting the group. But something is happening in Protestantism which lends new significance to the words "congregation" and "church" in the newspaper story. Protestantism is rediscovering the church. A steady flow of books on the doctrine of the church continues to move from the presses to the bookstores.[2] The meaning of the church is being discussed avidly

---

[1] *Minneapolis Morning Tribune*, Monday, August 7, 1961.

[2] See for example Conrad Bergendoff, *The One Holy Catholic Apostolic Church* (Rock Island: Augustana Book Concern, 1954) ; Ernest Best, *One Body in Christ* (London: S. P. C. K., 1955) ; Robert McAfee Brown, *The Significance of the Church* (Philadelphia: The Westminster Press, 1956) ; Suzanne de Dietrich, *The Witnessing Community* (Philadelphia: The Westminster Press, 1958) ; R. Newton Flew, *Jesus and His Church* (London: The Epworth Press, 1938) ; George Johnston, *The Doctrine of the Church in the New Testament* (Cambridge: University Press, 1943) ; Donald G. Miller, *The People of God* (London: SCM Press, 1959) ; Paul S. Minear, *Images of the Church in the New Testament* (Philadelphia: The Westminster Press, 1960) and *Jesus and His People* (New York: Association Press, 1956) ; Lesslie Newbigin, *The Household of God* (London: SCM Press, 1953) ; Anders Nygren, *Christ and His Church*, tr. Alan Carlsten (Philadelphia: The Westminster Press, 1956) ; Russell Shedd, *Man in Community* (London: The Epworth Press, 1958) ; W. A. Visser 't Hooft, *The Renewal of the Church* (London: SCM Press, 1956).

DR. SHAW is associate professor of religion at St. Olaf College, Northfield, Minn.

by youth conferences, lay discussion panels, pastoral institutes, and ecumenical gatherings. Yet it is possible to detect
a certain coolness toward all the church talk which is filling
the air. As always, there are some Protestants who speak
disdainfully of "the organized church." The recent rash of
church mergers moves many to cry alarm at burgeoning big-
ness and bureaucracy, and not without cause. A perennial
Protestant fear is that too much emphasis on the church may
lead in the direction of something uncomfortably similar to
the Roman ecclesiastical structure.

Basic to all such suspicions is the historically discredited
but still potent image of Luther and Calvin as emancipators
who cut men loose from all corporate ties, not the least of
which, so it is held, was the church.[3] It is not the purpose
here to advance the general argument that "the Church *is*
Christianity; and that the faith without community, the
fellowship of the One Body, would be a contradiction in
terms."[4] That argument has been advanced convincingly by
the authors whose works are cited in Note 2 and by many
others. Rather, the intention in the following pages is to
show that, when taken with full seriousness, the corporate
nature of Christianity must invade the very precinct where
popular Protestantism has always held its individualism to
be most self-evident and unassailable, namely, the area of
personal fellowship with Christ, or "the new life." That newness of life in Christ is not exclusively an individual matter
but has a decided corporate character will be substantiated
by a brief examination of four central concepts in the New
Testament: (1) the Holy Spirit, (2) Baptism, (3) the Lord's
Supper, and (4) the Christian hope. Supplementing the primary evidence of the New Testament will be some statements
taken from the writings of Martin Luther.

A few preliminary comments may prove helpful in direct-

---

3 Cf. J. S. Whale, *Christian Doctrine* (Cambridge: University Press, 1956), pp. 144-
149. See also the same author's *The Protestant Tradition* (Cambridge: University Press,
1955), p. 111. On p. 145 of the latter book Whale points out that Calvin devoted one-
third of the *Institutio* to the nature, order, powers, discipline, and ministry of the
Church.
4Whale, *The Protestant Tradition*, p. 320.

ing attention to the role of the church at the very inception of faith. Too often Protestant Christians have held that the church is a phenomenon making its appearance after a number of individuals have come to faith in Jesus Christ. Friedrich Schleiermacher provided a famous formulation of the latter point of view when he wrote: "The Christian Church takes shape through the coming together of regenerate individuals to form a system of mutual interaction and cooperation."[5] This statement contains a partial truth. The New Testament and all genuine Christian experience amply document the radical "I-thou" nature of man's answer to the call of Christ. It is evident that each man believes for himself, that no second party can take the step of faith for him. Individual answerability to God will always remain one of Protestantism's most cherished teachings.

What is less generally recognized, especially in periods of dominant individualism, is that the arena where the lonely man struggles with the summons of the Gospel is surrounded by a throng of believers whose witness to the trustworthiness of God in Christ plays a significant part in the individual's decision. One could even say that the lonely man is not really in the arena all by himself; others are there with him, and some of them have already responded to the invitation of the Gospel. To change the figure to one used by Luther, the church is "the mother who bears and fosters every individual Christian through the Word of God."[6]

The objection to Schleiermacher's definition of the church, then, is not that it makes mention of individual regeneration, but rather that it fails to recognize that the church is prior to individual faith. Without the church's proclamation of the Word of God and its corporate witness to the saving power of that Word, how would the individual be confronted with God's claim upon him? As Dr. Whale writes, "The Gospel of pardon reaches you and me through the mediation of the

---

5Friedrich Schleiermacher, *The Christian Faith*, eds. H. R. Mackintosh and J. S. Stewart (Edinburgh: T. & T. Clark, 1928), p. 532.
6Martin Luther, *The Large Catechism*, in *Triglot Concordia:* The Symbolic Books of the Ev. Lutheran Church (St. Louis: Concordia Publishing House, 1921), p. 689.

Christian society, the living body of believers in whose midst the redeeming Gospel of Christ goes out across the centuries and the continents."[7] To the objection that countless persons have come to faith in Christ apart from "the mediation of the Christian society," simply through the reading of the Bible, one must offer the reminder that "we receive the Bible from the hands of the Church."[8] Realizing how offensive such a statement is to a good many Protestant ears, the writer responsible for the phrase just quoted, C. H. Dodd, makes the following clarification:

> The Scriptures of the New Testament grew up within the life of the Church. Their selection out of a larger body of writings was a function of its growing corporate life, in response to a developing situation. Consequently the Church is prior to the Scriptures of the New Testament. On the other hand, the "covenant" ("testament") itself, that act of God which is attested in the Scriptures, is prior to the Church, for without it there is no Church. This mutual relation between Church and New Testament is fundamental.[9]

In the above preliminary comments an attempt has been made to articulate the fact that the Christian community has a great deal to do with the beginning of the life of faith. It will not do to relegate the role of the church to that part of the Christian life which follows the initial act of faith, as if faith is born independently and only subsequently seeks fellowship. It is now time to turn to the main contention of this discussion, namely, that the church is also integral to the continuing life of faith. The new life in Christ possesses a corporate character, as can be seen, first of all, in its relation to, and participation in, the Holy Spirit.

THE FELLOWSHIP OF, AND IN, THE SPIRIT

The teaching of the New Testament on the Holy Spirit is to be distinguished from that of the Old Testament by the

---

[7]Whale, *Christian Doctrine*, p. 128.
[8]C. H. Dodd, *The Bible Today* (Cambridge: University Press, 1952), p. 5.
[9]*Ibid.*, p. 8.

new fact of the bestowal of the Spirit upon the community as a whole, rather than upon selected individuals, as was the case in old Israel (cf. 1 Sam. 10:6, Mic. 3:8, Isa. 61:1, Ezek. 3:12, 14). It must be remembered that the sermon of Peter recorded in Acts 2:14-36, concluding with the bold declaration that "God has made him both Lord and Christ, this Jesus whom you crucified," was preached on the occasion of the Spirit's descent upon the gathered church. Here the Spirit has prompted the whole assembly of believers to confess Jesus as Lord and Christ; elsewhere in the New Testament (1 Cor. 12:3) the individual's confession of Jesus' lordship is also prompted by the Holy Spirit. In other words, the community's reception of the Spirit results in a corporate witness being given to the lordship of Jesus Christ. It would follow that the individual believer's witness is valid only if it corresponds with and shares in "the same Spirit" (1 Cor. 12:4) who descended on the church at Pentecost and impelled it to bear witness to the risen Christ.

Yet, modern Christianity has tended to make much of the individual's enlightenment by the Spirit, to the neglect of the historical and collective bestowal of the Spirit upon the church as a whole. The reasoning seems to be, following Schleiermacher, that when a number of individuals have separately partaken of the Spirit's power, they pool their impulses and insights and form a church. The new life in Christ, then, is also conceived of as a private exercise in spirituality. In popular religious language, the "spiritual life" has come to stand for those attitudes, feelings, and acts of devotion which the believer cultivates in his solitude. Each Christian is thought of as a separate vehicle of the Holy Spirit, as an independent bundle of spiritual energy free to make whatever disposition he prefers of the divine power of which he is the carrier.

Against this atomistic view of the Holy Spirit's activity, the New Testament pictures a historical community, the "body of Christ," the "fellowship of the Spirit," membership in which enables the individual to share in the life of the Spirit (2 Cor. 13:14, Phil. 2:1; cf. Acts 2:42).[10] That is, to be endowed with the Spirit is to be in on what Christ's new community is doing. Viewing life in the Spirit solely as an individual gift fails to do justice to the progress between the Old and the New Testaments. It simply extends the Old Testament idea to more people without sensing the new feature in the New Testament which is that now the entire community of which the believer is a member is energized by a divine power, a corporate gift characterizing the new community in the new age (Heb. 6:4-5).

The corporate reception of the Holy Spirit does not eliminate the need for personal appropriation of its power. Neither does it remove the "mutual interaction and co-operation" to which Schleiermacher referred. In fact, when it is recognized that the same Spirit motivates the individual and the community, there will be a greater experience of mutuality among the members. The important consideration is that the source of the community's new life of faith, obedience, love, and service is not to be found in scattered individuals with their varying degrees of intensity of spiritual experiences, but instead in the objective fact of the Spirit's presence in the community.

It is true that the Spirit-filled individual contributes to the building up of the community and to its effectiveness as God's instrument of service in this world. But the life of the Spirit also flows in the opposite direction: The individual receives impulses of the Christ-life from the community as he shares in its corporate existence, and in the strength of such assistance he is enabled to grow toward maturity of selfhood. This fact has seldom been noted and appreciated, precisely because Protestantism feels obliged to safeguard the individual's primacy as the recipient and bearer of spiritual power. In its well-intentioned zeal to have the individual face up to his personal responsibilities in the ongoing strug-

---

10L. S. Thornton, *The Common Life in the Body of Christ* (Westminster: Dacre Press, 1942), p. 69. This writer maintains that the Holy Spirit is not to be regarded as the subject who brings the believers together, but as the object in which they all share.

gle between God's truth and the forces of evil, Protestantism feeds the ego or increases the despair of the individual by urging him to think that all spiritual power must emanate from his own inner life. This individual also has the right to know that in the community's life there is power for him to appropriate, as Scripture makes clear by consistently setting the believer within the community, from which he draws his life.[11] Walther Eichrodt, an Old Testament scholar, puts the matter as follows:

> As a member of the people to whom God had revealed himself and to whom he had given his promises, the individual ventured to believe in God's power, wisdom and goodness also with respect to his own life.[12]

The New Testament expands and deepens the same principle in the relation between the body and the members. "If one member suffers, all suffer together; if one member is honored, all rejoice together" (1 Cor. 12:26). Similarly, while it is true that the Spirit bestows special gifts upon individuals, these are given "for the common good" (1 Cor. 12:7). Therefore there is every reason to rejoice as much in what the other members have been given as in the particular spiritual gift which I have been given, since whatever belongs to the body also belongs to me. By having a part in the community's common possession of the Spirit, the individual not only is allowed to develop his own spiritual gift; he is enriched by the totality of all the other gifts by virtue of his place in the body of Christ. The result of this mutual profiting among church members from one another's gifts is recognized by the apostle Paul as a strengthening of the fellowship.

Implicit in Paul's description of the body and its members is another benefit: the strengthening of individual selfhood. In view of the situation at Corinth in his day, Paul finds it

[11] Johannes Pedersen, *Israel: Its Life and Culture*, tr. Aslaug Möller (London: Oxford University Press, 1926), I-II, 259.
[12] Walther Eichrodt, *Theologie des Alten Testaments* (2nd ed.; Berlin: Evangelische Verlagsanstalt, 1948), III, 2.

most expedient to stress the role of individual endowments of the Spirit as contributing to "the common good." It is not the case that our times no longer see individuals excessively proud of their spirituality as those Corinthian church members were proud. The problem faced by Paul as he wrote to Corinth has a different focus in our day, however. Where Paul appealed for a true understanding of the body of Christ, the community, our dilemma is to restore individual integrity to lives threatened by all maner of conformist pressures, but to do so precisely by affirming the meaning of the church. We should learn from the apostle that nothing is gained by pitting individual against group; as far as Christ's followers are concerned, one becomes a true person, a true self, only as one lives and shares with others in the church, the body of Christ. This is often a humbling process, as human selfishness and aggressiveness come under the judgment of God's Word and the conscience is stirred by the probings of the divine Spirit. But there is also growth in faith and forbearance, mutual forgiveness, brotherly concern, all of which makes for the realization of genuine selfhood on the part of each member.

Too often the individual has been challenged to produce the Spirit-filled life in the strength of a kind of heroic inwardness. Instead, he ought to be assured that the Spirit's power flows through the organic life of the body and therefore can be experienced by him. Those who regard the Holy Spirit as the means for attaining to an exalted spiritual virtuosity find little encouragement in the New Testament where the emphasis falls instead on the whole community's participation in the Spirit (2 Cor. 13:14). The ordinary believer and the apparently exceptional believer have each been initiated into the life of the church through Baptism, which for either one means "the moment of his personal initiation into the sphere of the operation of the Holy Spirit."[13] Therefore all that the community is and has can be

---

[13] Alan Richardson, *An Introduction to the Theology of the New Testament* (London: SCM Press, 1958), p. 110. Published in U.S.A. by Harper & Row.

drawn upon by the individual members, for the common good, and for the enhancement of the meaning of personal existence.

The power of the Spirit is present in the community, but not all will avail themselves of it. There are marked differences in the individual responses to the workings of the Holy Spirit. That is why apostolic writers found it necessary to admonish their Christian friends to "walk by the Spirit" (Gal. 5:16) and to "maintain the unity of the Spirit" (Eph. 4:3), while warning them against grieving the Spirit (Eph. 4:30) or quenching the Spirit (1 Thess. 5:19). Paul clearly combines the idea of the gift of the Spirit as that which makes Christian living possible with the appeal to Christians to exercise that gift: "If we live by the Spirit, let us also walk by the Spirit" (Gal. 5:25; cf. Rom. 8:13-14).

It was stated earlier that Protestant Christians have too readily assumed that the one dimension of Christianity which is most obviously "individual" is the believer's inner communion with Christ. While this intimate fellowship between the Christian and his Lord is eminently personal, the contention being made here is that it is more than individual; it is also communal.[14] In fact, when the new life of the Christian is seen in its proper communal framework, a new and inviting light is cast on the Christian's fellowship with God in Christ. The believing member going in and out among his fellows in the church receives support and insight which makes his "individual" fellowship with Christ a much deeper experience. The man who shares in "the new life of the Spirit" (Rom. 7:6) becomes an authentic specimen of individual selfhood because he nourishes his own life from the fellowship of the Holy Spirit. A sentence by G. Ernest Wright is appropriate here:

The biblical story must not be interpreted as the progressive emancipation of the individual, but instead as God's

---

[14]Åke V. Ström, *Vetekornet: Studier över Individ och Kollektiv i Nya Testamentet* (Stockholm: Svenska Kyrkans Diakonistyrelses Bokförlag, 1944), pp. 112, 220-221.

action in history to create a community in which the responsible individual finds his true being.[15]

THE COMPANY OF THE BAPTIZED

The New Testament idea of Baptism furnishes additional and concrete support for the thesis that the individual becomes a true person by incorporation within the Christian community. Baptism, as Richardson has put it, is initiation into the sphere of the operation of the Holy Spirit. "For by one Spirit we were all baptized into one body—Jews or Greeks, slaves or free—and all were made to drink of one Spirit" (1 Cor. 12:13). The body was there first, says Paul, and by Baptism the individual is brought into it. In *The Large Catechism* Luther similarly speaks of "Baptism, by which we are first received into the Christian Church."[16] The point seems simple enough—the community precedes the individual—but much of Protestantism will not have it so. Historically, the idea of the church as a voluntary association of believers stems principally from the left wing of the Reformation but, as the popularity of Schleiermacher's definition of the church as the coming together of regenerated individuals shows, great segments of Protestantism have exalted the individual soul as the primary religious entity, quite out of keeping with what the Reformation brought to light concerning the church.[17]

Nothing could be more indisputable than the intrinsically personal, even individual, significance of Baptism. In the Sacrament of Baptism the candidate's name is solemnly linked with the name of the triune God. It is impossible to imagine a more radically personal transaction. At the same time Baptism offers a vivid instance of the significant interrelationship between the individual and the community into

---

[15] G. Ernest Wright, *The Biblical Doctrine of Man in Society* (London: SCM Press, 1954), p. 97. Published in U.S.A. by Alec R. Allenson, Inc.
[16] *Triglot Concordia*, p. 733.
[17] Martin E. Marty, *A Short History of Christianity* (Cleveland and New York: Meridian Books, © 1958, The World Publishing Co.), p. 216: "His [Luther's] own high and pervasive view of the Church is incompatible with the individualistic rewriting of Reformation history of modern times. The Reformers did not intend to repudiate the communal and churchly character of God's redemptive activity. They did not intend to invent autonomous man." Used by permission of the publishers.

which he is received. Baptism is possible only where the Word of God and the church are present. When, in Baptism, the individual is given a new identity, it is an identity established historically through God's new covenant with his people in Christ's death and resurrection, and mediated in the present as the gracious Word of promise through Christ's believing church. To use a New Testament figure, the baptized one becomes a member of "the household of God" (Eph. 2:19). Thus, while Baptism signifies that this particular person is brought into a saving relationship with God, at the same time it signifies that from this moment on he carries the mark of a specific religious community. His very personal existence in Christ therefore is a reflection of a profound social fact. He is not a baptized Christian first and a member of the church second. The one fact of Baptism immediately and inevitably has corporate significance.

The communal significance of Baptism is further supported when one considers that the famous Pauline phrase "in Christ" is equivalent to "in the church." A number of years ago the German scholar Adolf Deissmann developed the Pauline "in Christ" concept along highly individualistic and mystical lines,[18] while later scholars have rightly demonstrated that the phrase is to be understood in keeping with the early church's strong awareness of Christ's presence in the fellowship.[19] Therefore, when Paul writes, "Do you not know that all of us who have been baptized into Christ Jesus were baptized into his death? We were buried therefore with him by baptism into death, so that as Christ was raised from the dead by the glory of the Father, we too might walk in newness of life" (Rom. 6:3-4), his plural pronouns ("you," "we," "us") take on special meaning for the church. To be "in Christ" or to be brought by Baptism "into Christ Jesus" are phrases meaning that the individual belongs to a sphere

---

[18]Adolf Deissmann, *Die neutestamentliche Formel "in Christo Jesu"* (Marburg, 1892). Cf. also Deissmann, *Paul: A Study in Social and Religious History*, tr. William E. Wilson (New York: Harper & Brothers Publishers, 1957), pp. 140 ff.

[19]Ernst Käsemann, *Leib und Leib Christi* (Tübingen: J. C. B. Mohr [Paul Siebeck], 1933), p. 183 ; Ernst Percy, *Der Leib Christi* (Lund: C. W. K. Gleerup, 1942), p. 44.

of power dominated by the risen Christ.[20] Percy says that "baptized into one body" (1 Cor. 12:13) is analogous to being baptized "into Christ" (Rom. 6:3).[21]

The connection between Baptism and "the new life" might appear to be a strained one since Baptism is naturally and correctly held to be the initiatory rite whereas faith and obedience continue throughout the individual's earthly existence. But if Baptism is understood in its eschatological meaning, that is, as a continuing reality extending to the believer's death and on to Christ's return, it will be seen that Baptism has very much to do with the Christian's entire earthly struggle. One thinks at once of Martin Luther's tactic of fending off severe assaults by the devil by writing the words "I am baptized" on the table in front of him. A glance at Luther's "Treatise on Baptism" (1519) discloses the Reformer's profound understanding of Baptism as something spanning a person's whole life and extending through death itself. Luther writes:

> The sacrament, or sign, of baptism is quickly over, as we plainly see. But the thing it signifies, viz., the spiritual baptism, the drowning of sin, lasts so long as we live, and is completed only in death. . . . Therefore this life is nothing else than a spiritual baptism which does not cease till death. . . .[22]

Luther was particularly grateful for the power which Baptism furnished the believer in his struggles against sin. The baptized man should not expect to be free from evil thoughts, temptations, and sins, nor should he despair when he finds himself incapable of pure acts. His recourse is to "remember his baptism, and comfort himself joyfully with it, since God has there bound Himself to slay his sin for him."[23] But remembering one's Baptism does not, for Lu-

---

20Ernest Best, *One Body in Christ* (London: S. P. C. K., 1955), makes use of the term "corporate personality," made famous by H. Wheeler Robinson, in describing the communal nature of being "in Christ." See p. 20 of Best's book.
21Percy, *op. cit.*, p. 16.
22"A Treatise on Baptism," *Works of Martin Luther*, The Philadelphia Edition (Philadelphia: Muhlenberg Press, 1943), I, 57.
23*Ibid.*, p. 62.

ther, imply passivity over against sin and temptation. The Treatise makes it very clear that the believer strives mightily against sin, recognizing his evil inclination as sin and struggling against it "in many trials, works, and sufferings." Those who refuse to take up the battle against evil forfeit their chance of being forgiven "because they do not live according to their baptism and covenant."[24]

It may now be asked: "But what does this individual remembering of one's Baptism and striving against sin from the strength of the baptismal covenant have to do with the church's role in the believer's spiritual development?" The answer is not supplied so much in a given New Testament text as in the basic fact that "to be in Christ" is the same as "to be in the church."[25] The first century Christians with their strong sense of corporate solidarity did not feel the need to present arguments in support of the church's role in their lives. They would not, in fact, understand our assumption that "private devotional life" and "church activity" are somehow separate qualities of Christian existence. The appeal "to lead a life worthy of the calling to which you have been called" in Ephesians 4 is followed immediately by the reminder that "there is one body and one Spirit . . . one Lord, one faith, one baptism" (Eph. 4:1, 4-5). The individual and the congregation alike derive the capacity to lead worthy lives from those great redemptive facts which belong to the common experience of the church, including Baptism.

Here it may be profitable to pause for a brief review of what has been said thus far. The aim of this entire discussion is to show that "the new life" in Christ, which in modern parlance is called variously "the Christian life" or "fellowship with Christ" or even "the spiritual life," is fundamentally not the cultivation of individual inwardness, but rather the believer's participation in the corporate life of the Christian community. Furthermore, there is also the correl-

24*Ibid.*, p. 64.
25Käsemann, *loc. cit.*

ative aim of suggesting that placing the primary emphasis on the church and its corporate gifts, far from stifling individual spiritual life and rendering it passive, actually supplies the correct biblical understanding of personal selfhood which, it is seen, is much richer and more promising when comprehended in community than can ever be the case when man is interpreted as an isolated being who pursues the new life entirely within the domain of his private meditations.

The first set of observations had to do with the concept of the Holy Spirit. The New Testament shows little interest in individual specialists in spirituality, though it does recognize that not all believers will respond to the urgings of the Spirit in the same way or to the same degree. The main emphasis is on the participation of all believers in the Holy Spirit, suggesting that individuals come to realize their true selves only as they avail themselves of that which God has bestowed upon his church in the Spirit's presence and power.

The second major instance of the corporate character of the new life was Baptism. Baptism is, of course, a profoundly personal matter, as seen in the fact that the candidate's name is connected with God's own name as the Sacrament is received. At the same time, and without lessening but rather strengthening the personal significance of Baptism, the New Testament points to the social dimension which makes this Sacrament what it is: the rite whereby individuals become members of the church. Furthermore, Baptism's eschatological nature means that the baptized person through his whole life draws upon the promise received in Baptism and in so doing strengthens his faith. Yet he is not alone in his struggle against sin and unbelief, since as long as he is "in Christ" he is by that same fact a member of the church, which is Christ's body.

THE FELLOWSHIP OF THE TABLE

A third focus of the corporate life in Christ is the Lord's Supper. Here again, as in the case of Baptism, one finds that what the assembled community experiences makes for the enrichment of the individual, but still the corporate reality is predominant. One is forced to marvel at how Protestantism, through neglect of the Supper's intrinsic corporate intention, has so thoroughly "individualized" its benefits. Theological disputes concerning the meaning of Holy Communion too often seem to presuppose that the first consideration is to determine the exact nature of the transaction between Christ and the individual. It should be noted with respect to all of the New Testament concepts being discussed in these pages—the Holy Spirit, Baptism, the Lord's Supper, the Christian hope—that the very nature of life in community precludes the drawing of sharp lines between the corporate and individual spheres. But as one seeks to apply the insights of the New Testament to the conditions in present-day church life, it is evident that certain disproportions call for corrective comment. Such would seem to be the case in conspicuous measure when the very Sacrament which is corporate by self-designation, Holy Communion, has become encircled with pious ideas and feelings of the most blatantly individualistic sort. The notion of "private communion" is one example.

The problem of "divisions" to which Paul addresses himself in First Corinthians 11 has much in common with modern habits of viewing the Lord's Supper as a means to individual spiritual gratification. The worshippers at Corinth were guilty of denying the spirit of mutuality among the members of the congregation. So as Paul issues his rebuke he begins pointedly with the remark, "when you assemble *as a church*" (Greek: ἐν ἐκκλησία, 1 Cor. 11:18). Whatever the exact nature of the reprehensible conduct was, Paul disapproved because it was essentially selfish and unmindful of the unity of the congregation. "When you meet together, it is not the Lord's Supper that you eat. For in eating, each one goes ahead with his own meal, and one is hungry and another is drunk" (1 Cor. 11:20-21).

Later in the same chapter appears another passage scoring the lack of regard for the oneness of the congregation: "For any one who eats and drinks without discerning the *body* [Greek: σῶμα] eats and drinks judgment upon himself. That is why many of you are weak and ill, and some have died" (1 Cor. 11:29-30). The historical circumstances occasioning this passage are not entirely clear, but the principle for which Paul is contending is both clear and important: a proper participation in the Lord's Supper requires that the worshippers be aware that in this sacramental action the one body of Jesus which was given in death on the cross is now known and experienced by the followers of Christ in his risen body, the church. It is not every man for himself; taking part in the sacred meal calls for the discerning of the body. The latter cannot be a divided body and still be the body of Christ. Those who fail to discern the body act as if each believer were entitled to a greedy, independent appropriation of the Lord's Supper, disregarding the fact that Christ's death and resurrection brought into being a community where the members have a loving regard for one another.

In the light of the above, one may justifiably question the attitude of those who attend the Lord's Supper for the exclusive purpose of gaining private spiritual benefits. The nature of the issue is such that no one would presume to level specific criticisms; nevertheless, the impression remains strong that much of the preaching, thinking, and feeling regarding Holy Communion does tend to emphasize onesidedly the individual devotional value of the experience, whether Communion is received at the altar rail, at the communion table, or in the pew.

On the positive side, Paul states in First Corinthians 10: "Because there is one loaf, we who are many are one body, for we all partake of the same loaf" (v. 17). Not only must Christians be cautioned against making the Lord's Supper a private affair; they must also be encouraged to claim the kind of benefits from the Supper which this particular Sacrament by its corporate nature is so admirably suited to bestow. Luther's "Treatise on the Blessed Sacrament" provides some splendid comments in exposition of this idea:

> The significance or purpose of this sacrament is the fellowship of all saints, whence it derives its common name *synaxis* or *communio*, that is, fellowship; and *communicare* means to take part in this fellowship, or as we say, to go to the sacrament, because Christ and all saints are one spiritual body, just as the inhabitants of a city are one community and body, each citizen being a member of the other and a member of the entire city. . . . To receive the bread and wine of this sacrament, then, is nothing else than to receive a sure sign of this fellowship and incorporation with Christ and all saints.[26]

It is profitable to follow Luther's thinking somewhat further along the line of the mutual interaction which takes place in this Sacrament. In the next set of quotations to be given Luther mentions in turn what the believer receives from the fellowship, how the believer is able to share his burdens with the fellowship and, finally, that the believer also assumes the burdens of others:

> In this sacrament, therefore, God Himself gives through the priest a sure sign to man, to show that, in like manner, he shall be united with Christ and His saints and have all things in common with them; that Christ's sufferings and life shall be his own, together with the lives and sufferings of all the saints. . . .[27]
> If any one be in despair, if he be distressed by his sinful conscience or terrified by death, or have any other burden on his heart, and desire to be rid of them all, let him go joyfully to the sacrament of the altar and lay down his grief in the midst of the congregation and seek help from the entire company of the spiritual body. . . .[28]
> When you have partaken of this sacrament, therefore, or

---

[26]"A Treatise Concerning the Blessed Sacrament of the Holy and True Body of Christ and Concerning the Brotherhoods," *Works of Martin Luther*, The Philadelphia Edition (Philadelphia: Muhlenberg Press, 1943), II, 10-11.
[27]Luther, "A Treatise Concerning the Blessed Sacrament," p. 12.
[28]*Ibid.*, p. 13.

desire to partake of it, you must in turn also share the
misfortunes of the congregation. . . . There your heart
must go out in love and devotion and learn that this
sacrament is a sacrament of love, and that love and service are given you and you again must render love and
service to Christ and His needy ones. . . . We on our part
must make others' evil our own, if we desire Christ and
His saints to make our evil their own; then will the
fellowship be complete and justice be done to the sacrament. For the sacrament has no blessing and significance
unless love grows daily and so changes a man that he
is made one with all others.[29]

An examination of the accounts of the Last Supper which
Jesus held with his disciples discloses some conspicuous
features emphasizing the corporate nature of the event
itself and its corporate significance for successive generations. The mention of the word "covenant" is especially tell-
ing in this respect. "This is my blood of the covenant, which
is poured out for many" (Mark 14:24; cf. Matt. 26:28 and
1 Cor. 11:25). The attentive reader is at once reminded of
God's historical covenant with his people (cf. Ex. 24:8), and
Paul's version of the institution of the Lord's Supper reports
that Jesus spoke of his approaching sacrifice as "the new
covenant" in which his followers share through their reception of his body and blood (1 Cor. 11:24-26).[30]

Giving added force to the distinctly communal character
of the Sacrament of the Altar are the Lord's words in Matthew, "Drink of it, all of you" (Matt. 26:27) and the report
by Mark, ". . . and they all drank of it" (Mark 14:23),
coupled with the promise that the blood of the covenant "is
poured out for many" (Matt. 26:28; Mark 14:24). It is
plain, then, that the believing participant at the Lord's Table
finds himself linked with God's redemptive, covenant-estab-
lishing work throughout history and thus with all those who
belong to God's people. That there is a profoundly personal,
indeed intimate, relationship with Christ expected by the

---

[29]*Ibid.*, pp. 13-17.
[30]F. W. Dillistone, *The Structure of the Divine Society* (London: Lutterworth Press,
1951), pp. 77-79.

communicant as he receives the Sacrament is entirely proper; but the Scriptures also testify to the broader realities of history and the covenant people as intrinsically related to the fellowship of the Lord's Table.

In a day when the leaders of the churches are working diligently to implement effective cooperation between denominations, and mergers are being projected and realized on larger and smaller scales, it is essential that Christians be helped to lay hold of the ecumenical reality which faces them in the local, concrete form of their own congregation's celebration of Holy Communion. It is not a matter of adding some extra trapping to local communion practice; certainly it is not a case of introducing the corporate appreciation of the Sacrament as a novel dimension. The Sacrament of the Lord's Supper is inherently a community rite, and the communal or fellowship aspect has always been present, even if overlooked. What is needed is explicit preaching and teaching which will enable the membership of the church to recover that experience of oneness with Christ and all his people to which the Sacrament of the Altar points them.

The stronger the sense of oneness in the congregation, the healthier becomes the faith of the individual. Instead of going to the Sacrament with the attitude of one who secretly dreads a terrifying private interview with the Almighty, the believer will joyfully lay his burdens and anxieties upon the assembled congregation and take with him from the communion table the comfort and fortification of the entire church's faith and devotion. In the words of Luther:

> Though I am a sinner and have fallen, though this or that misfortune has befallen me, I will go to the sacrament to receive a sign from God that I have on my side Christ's righteousness, life and sufferings, with all holy angels and all the blessed in heaven, and all pious men on earth. If I die, I am not alone in death; if I suffer, they suffer with me. I have shared all my misfortune with Christ and the saints, since I have a sure sign of their love toward me.[31]

---
[31] Luther, "A Treatise Concerning the Blessed Sacrament," p. 13.

Such an experience, one cannot insist too strongly, is of one piece with what is usually thought of as the individual's spiritual life. The fear that a lively interest in the blessings offered by Christ in the Sacrament will jeopardize the intensity of personal inwardness is both unnecessary and harmful. The Christian who regularly nourishes his faith at the communion table may become less of an "individual," in the usual sense, but he does become more of a "person." That is, instead of regarding himself as a self-contained unit set apart from others, he will rejoice in the growing discovery that as a "person," a free creature of God charged with accepting responsibility for his own actions but also blessed with the privilege of entering into relations with other human beings, he can know the development of selfhood which comes within the creative fellowship with other selves. Besides being unique because of its divine origin, the church is also unique because it simultaneously maintains both personal freedom and genuine community at the highest level.[32] That which makes a man a unique person is not minimized in order to produce harmonious conformity.[33] On the contrary, membership in the church's organic life makes possible an enhancement of personal life which could never be realized if the individual were to tread the lonely path of spiritual isolation, however zealous his efforts.[34] Many who are "weak and ill" (1 Cor. 11:30) in Christian congregations today would become strong and well if they went to the Lord's Table confidently believing with the author of Colossians that the goal of presenting "every man mature in Christ" (Col. 1:28) is meant to be reached through the operation of the Word of God in and through the church. And the ministry of the Word is not complete without the enacted Word in the Sacrament.

32Ström, *loc. cit.*

33J. S. Stewart, *A Man in Christ* (New York: Harper & Brothers Publishers, 1935), p. 166: "Union with Christ, so far from obliterating the believer's personal qualities and characteristics, throws these into greater relief."

34"The personal is exactly that which constitutes the richness of the community's life," writes Hugo Odeberg in "The Individualism of Today and the Concept of the Church in the New Testament," *This is the Church*, ed. Anders Nygren, tr. Carl C. Rasmussen (Philadelphia: Muhlenberg Press, 1952), p. 68.

THE COMMON HOPE

By this time the reader can easily anticipate the direction of any remarks to be made concerning the Christian hope: the promises of the New Testament pointing to the future have not merely an individual but also a corporate reference. Such an anticipation is basically correct, but one must face at the outset the fact that death is a uniquely individual matter. An evident paradox presents itself at this point, for where Luther was quoted above as saying, "If I die, I am not alone," a sermon which he preached at Wittenberg in Lent of 1522 begins with the words:

> The challenge of death comes to us all, and no one can die for another. Every one must fight his own battle with death by himself, alone. We can shout into one another's ears, but every one must be prepared finally to meet death alone. I will not be with you then, nor you with me.[35]

The paradox must be permitted to stand: man faces the last enemy, death, quite alone; at the same time, the fellowship of believers to which he belongs is there to shout encouragement in his ears, to remind him that God is faithful at the moment when death's terrors are causing him to doubt.

The New Testament obviously displays a more fully developed concept of man's destiny after death, expressed in the doctrine of the resurrection of the body, than does the Old Testament. Despite suggestive passages like Job 19:25-26, Isaiah 25:8 and 26:19,[36] Daniel 12:2, and Psalm 73:24, which point in the direction of resurrection and personal life after death, the predominant Old Testament view is that when death comes, a man is gathered to his people (Gen. 49:29), he goes to Sheol, the abode of the dead (Gen. 37:35, Ps. 6:5; 31:17; 139:8).[37] Later Judaism developed a belief in resurrection which the Pharisees promoted (Acts 23:6-8). According to the New Testament, at the center of the Christian

---

[35] *Works of Martin Luther*, II, 391.
[36] Bernhard Anderson notes that Isaiah 26:19 is "the first clear reference in the Old Testament to the resurrection of the individual." Anderson, *Understanding the Old Testament* (Englewood Cliffs, N. J.: Prentice Hall, Inc., 1957), p. 519.
[37] *The Westminster Dictionary of the Bible*, ed. John D. Davis (rev. ed.; Philadelphia: The Westminster Press, 1924), p. 235.

hope is belief in the resurrection (1 Peter 1:3-5), and the various images used by the writers clearly imply the personal quality of life beyond the grave (cf. Luke 23:43, 1 Cor. 15:23, 35-50, Rev. 22:3-4). The contrast between the earlier Old Testament view, which conceived of the individual as passing at death into a rather drab collective existence among the shades, and the fully developed New Testament idea of personal fellowship with Christ after death—this contrast would have been interpreted a few decades ago as additional evidence for the superiority of the New Testament's "individualism" over the "collectivism" of the Old Testament.

As a Swedish scholar, Åke V. Ström, has shown, the development to be traced through the biblical literature is not one from collectivism to individualism, but rather one from an impersonal collectivism to a personalistic collectivism.[38] The communal aspects of faith and hope are present in both Old and New Testament; the difference in the latter is that the meaning of personal selfhood becomes decisively etched out through the life, death, and resurrection of Jesus Christ. Ström observes that since the Christian is a member of a personalistic collectivity, the church, he must face squarely the responsibility for what he does with his life, being accountable to God, and, further, his personal identity and integrity continue after death.[39] Second Corinthians 5:10 brings out the greater accountability which is laid on the member of Christ's body: "For we must all appear before the judgment seat of Christ, so that each one may receive good or evil, according to what he has done in the body." That is, since these words are addressed to church members, it is clear that personal responsibility is not lessened through association with the corporate people of God; it is intensified.[40]

Thus far the discussion of the Christian hope has centered on the point that death and the judgment which fol-

---

38Ström, *loc. cit.*
39Ström, *loc. cit.*
40Nils A. Dahl, *Das Volk Gottes* (Oslo: Jacob Dybwad, 1941), p. 249.

lows are inescapably personal events. It is needful to establish this point lest misunderstanding arise over the corporate character of the Christian hope. As a matter of fact, the New Testament presents its teachings on the hope primarily with reference to the Christian community (*"we have been born anew to a living hope"*—1 Peter 1:3). All men will be confronted with their personal histories and judged accordingly, but those who belong to Christ by faith, i.e., the redeemed church, will receive the inheritance which God has prepared for his own people (Matt. 25:34). Where non-biblical thinking conceives of existence beyond death as something guaranteed by man's immortality, the New Testament writers ask their readers to cling in faith to the promises which God has given his people. Because there is a blessed future awaiting the church, the believer finds his comfort in identifying himself with the hopeful community.

The Christian hope as a function of the community should not surprise anyone who has reflected upon the consistently corporate eschatology of the entire Bible. That is, the people of God as a definite social unit is always in the foreground, from the earliest promises to Abraham (Gen. 12:1-3) to the new Jerusalem pictured in the Book of Revelation (21:1-4). At each stage in the unfolding redemptive process God indicates to his people that a greater day is in store for them. Intense eschatological expectations at various points in biblical history produced books like Daniel and Revelation, both of which depict the triumph of God's people over the enemies (cf. Dan. 7:23-27; Rev. 20:7-10). Even though the New Testament writers avoid the attempt to offer detailed descriptions of the new life with God after death, they do make use of imagery which is markedly social rather than individual. For example, Paul writes that "our commonwealth [Greek: πολίτευμα] is in heaven, and from it we await a Savior, the Lord Jesus Christ" (Phil. 3:20). The First Epistle of Peter, often called "The Epistle of Hope,"[41] is ad-

41Cf. A. M. Hunter, *Introducing the New Testament* (Philadelphia: The Westminster Press, 1946), p. 98. By permission.

dressed "to the exiles of the dispersion" (1 Peter 1:1), a conscious effort to identify the Christian church as the heir to the ancient promises given to Israel.

It should be noted here that the term "eschatology" cannot be taken to refer exclusively to the last things, i.e., the resurrection of the dead, the return of Christ, the final judgment, and the like. Eschatology in the New Testament sense actually has reference to the totality of the new process set in motion by the life, ministry, death, resurrection, and ascension of Jesus Christ, and continuing with the coming of the Holy Spirit as the effective power of the new age (cf. Heb. 6:5), and the subsequent life of the church. Thus when the Fourth Gospel reports Jesus as saying, "He who believes in the Son has eternal life" (John 3:36), the present tense of the verb signifies that faith in Jesus places a man within the new age of life which Jesus has inaugurated. Eternal life is a present reality. Similarly, in the Synoptic Gospels the kingdom of God is regarded as a present fact as well as something to come in the future (cf. Mark 1:15).

For the individual Christian, then, the Christian hope is not a pious wish concerning future happiness; instead, it is a fact which has already been experienced in the life of the church, the community which worships the risen Lord. The gift of the Holy Spirit constitutes the guarantee that the promises of God will be fulfilled (2 Cor. 1:22; cf. also 5:5). "In him you also, who have heard the word of truth, the gospel of your salvation, and have believed in him, were sealed with the promised Holy Spirit, which is the guarantee of our inheritance until we acquire possession of it, to the praise of his glory" (Eph. 1:13-14).

In stressing that the Christian hope is corporate as well as individual, it is not a question of ranking the two aspects in importance. Neither does one wish to take anything away from certain great biblical words of comfort (e.g., John 11:25-26) which have ministered hope and confidence to generations of individual believers. The central contention is that the Christian hope is only partially apprehended when the believer limits the application of Scripture's promises for the future to himself and his own destiny.[42] He can be reassured concerning his own future because in this life he has been incorporated into the fellowship of the Holy Spirit, the body of Christ, which, as a body, is destined to be gathered with Christ and all the saints in an eternal fellowship. In a study of Paul's theology as traced through the various ways the apostle employs the concept of "the body," John A. T. Robinson writes:

> Christians should be the last people to be found clinging to the wrecks of an atomistic individualism, which has no foundation in the Bible. For their hope does not lie in escape from collectivism: it lies in the resurrection of the body—that is to say, in the redemption, transfiguration, and ultimate supersession of one solidarity by another.[43]

To sum up, the new life in Christ has a corporate character. Unfortunately, the reigning conviction in Protestant circles[44] has been that vigorous Christianity is to be realized only by ceaseless pressure on the individual to intensify his efforts. "It all goes back to the individual" is a pious maxim which has long enjoyed considerable standing. In the pages of this discussion the plea has been entered to announce the Gospel of community existence to the struggling individual, instead of haranguing him with the Law of individual piety. For it is truly part of the Christian Gospel to let people know that Christ has delivered men from isolation. Therefore the individual is not alone in his endeavor to realize the Spirit's power in his life because the Spirit is primarily the gift of the risen Christ to the church. He is not alone in seeking to realize his full self because in Holy Baptism he is incor-

---

[42]Paul Althaus, "Eschatology," *A Handbook of Christian Theology* (Cleveland and New York: Meridian Books, © 1958, The World Publishing Co.), p. 102: "Christian hope is concerned with the future of every human being; however, it is not solely preoccupied with this. Although concerned with us as individuals, God's action nevertheless transpires in such a way that we are called, through Jesus Christ, into a communion which is Christ's Church."

[43]John A. T. Robinson, *The Body: A Study in Pauline Theology* (London: SCM Press, 1952), p. 9. Published in U.S.A. by Alec R. Allenson, Inc.

[44]Here and elsewhere the author directs his comments to Protestantism only because as a Protestant himself he knows that part of Christendom better.

porated into the new community of Christ which furnishes him with a new identity and gives him access to the spiritual riches of a historical fellowship with which God has made an enduring covenant. Nor is he alone in his consciousness of being unworthy to taste the bread and wine of the Lord's Table, for the gathered assembly with whom the risen Christ is present shares his fears and misgivings with him while at the same time extending the strength of its corporate life to each individual member. Finally, even though the individual must face death alone, he still has the help of the congregation, which reminds him that the body of Christ as a whole is the recipient of God's promise of an eternal fellowship.

It has always been difficult for Protestantism to overcome the persistent individualism which has been so much in evidence throughout its later history, even though the Reformers themselves were anything but champions of individualism. The past decades, however, have seen an encouraging trend in the direction of a new appreciation for the church, both in biblical scholarship and in practical church life. There are danger signs that these gains may be wiped out before they are firmly established. New versions of autonomous man are appearing, whether one reads the works of existentialist theologians or follows the course of the current psychological analysis of Christian experience. In the long run, existentialism and psychology will contribute to a better understanding of man's situation within various corporate structures, it is to be hoped. The present discussion has dealt with the Christian man as a member of the church and has contended that the way to genuine selfhood is to be found in the fellowship of the people of God, where corporate experience enriches individual existence and brings it to fulfillment.

II

Community and the Church

KENT S. KNUTSON

Community was the key word used in original Reformation thought to describe the nature of the church. For Luther, the two expressions "holy Christian church" and "communion of saints" in the Apostles' Creed were identical. He believed that the latter phrase was an addition to the Creed and intended by the ancient church as an explication of the meaning of church. The church to him is the *communio sanctorum*, the sanctified community.[1] The classic Reformation confessions, Anglican and Reformed as well as Lutheran, carry forward the same idea. "The Church is the congregation of saints, in which the Gospel is rightly taught and the Sacraments are rightly administered," states the Augsburg Confession, the universal and fundamental confession in world Lutheranism.[2]

The question that we shall put is this: How is the relationship between community and church understood today? We shall use the Lutherans as a case study. They have a more conscious and homogeneous commitment to the original definition of the Reformation than do other Protestant

[1] One of the finest contributions of the present Luther research into this aspect of Luther's thought is Paul Althaus, *Communio Sanctorum* (München: Chr. Kaiser Verlag, 1929). The primary work was done by Karl Holl, *Gesammelte Aufsätze zur Kirchengeschichte*, Vol. I: *Luther*, "Die Entstehung von Luthers Kirchenbegriff" (Tübingen: J. C. B. Mohr, 1932).
[2] *Book of Concord* (St. Louis: Concordia Publishing House, 1922), p. 13.

DR. KNUTSON is associate professor of systematic theology at Luther Theological Seminary, St. Paul, Minn.

37

groups and so are more easily analyzable. All Lutherans accept the above definition and claim fidelity to its meaning. We shall argue that despite this fact various patterns of relationships are manifest in the Lutheran tradition which demonstrate that the understanding of community in Protestantism is pluralistic. The four leading schools of thought in present-day Lutheranism will be used to illustrate this argument: repristination theology, pietism, Lundensian theology, and neo-confessionalism.

We shall first present the understanding of the church as it is explained by leading representatives of the four points of view. In doing so, we shall limit ourselves to the picture of church as seen through the basic category of community. Second, we shall address four questions to each of them: (1) What creates the church? That is, what is it that makes the church the church? (2) What kind of community is the church? (3) What is the relationship between the individual and this community? (4) What is the relationship between this community and the goal of the Christian religion? Or, to phrase it in another way, what does the church have to do with salvation?

But first a brief look at some of the ideas in original Lutheranism.

THE CHURCH AS COMMUNITY IN LUTHER AND THE CONFESSIONS

Luther is often quoted as saying that the idea of the church is so simple that a seven-year-old child could understand it.[3] In that delightful moment Luther brushed aside his own great struggle in arriving at his understanding. "No idea was more important in Luther's whole work than that of the church,"[4] and no idea more difficult to clarify after a thousand years of departure from the biblical concept. Even the word "church" seemed to have lost its useful-

---

3*Ibid.*, p. 148.
4Wilhelm Pauck, *The Heritage of the Reformation* (Boston: Beacon Press, 1950), p. 26. Dr. Pauck is probably the leading authority on Luther in this country.

ness. He discovered that the popular mind thought of either the church building or the institutional and organizational aspects when the German *Kirche* was mentioned. *Kirche* in the German Bible is the translation of the Greek ἐκκλησία, which strictly translated means assembly or gathering. Luther maintained that this meaning would be retained better in German if the word ἐκκλησία were translated "congregation" or, best of all and most clearly, "holy Christendom." The Latin *communio* he preferred to be translated *Gemeinde*, congregation or community. To make it even more simple, he would have liked to have the Creed read: "I believe that there is a holy Christian people," and let it go at that.[5]

The church was understood by Luther to be an object of faith for ". . . as this rock (Christ) is invisible and only to be grasped by faith, so, too, the church (apart from sin) must be spiritual and invisible, to be grasped only by faith."[6] As evidence of this basic orientation of his thought, Luther often used the words "spiritual," "inward," "invisible," "internal" when speaking of the church. He did not mean by this that the church was an abstract idea and therefore lacking in reality. Reacting strongly to the accusation that his church was only a "cloudland," a Platonic idea, he said: "When I have made the Church a spiritual assembly, you have insultingly taken me to mean that I would build a church as Plato builds a state that never was."[7]

The church, though spiritual, was nevertheless real and visible. Parallel with the above phrases are those he used to describe the church as "corporal," "outward," "visible," "external." He enumerated the visible signs of the church on many occasions. His treatise "On the Councils and the Church" is explicit in its listing of the marks of the church

---

[5]*Book of Concord*, trans. T. G. Tappert, J. Pelikan, R. H. Fischer, A. D. Piepkorn (Philadelphia: Muhlenberg Press, 1959), pp. 35 ff. Some of Luther's clearest thoughts concerning the church are elucidated in his Large Catechism. This is the best translation.

[6]Luther, as quoted by Gordon Rupp, *The Righteousness of God* (London: Hodder and Stoughton, 1953), p. 317. Some of the best modern interpretations of Luther have been by non-Lutherans. Dr. Rupp happens to be an English Methodist.

[7]*Ibid.*

which everyone can see.[8] There are at least seven marks: the preaching of the Word, the Sacrament of Baptism, the Sacrament of the Altar, the keys of Christian discipline and forgiveness, a called ministry, public assembly for worship, and the suffering of the Christian for his faith. Most important of all is the community itself, consisting of people of flesh and blood.

Luther struggled to maintain a dialectic tension between the two descriptive words "visible" and "invisible." That which creates the church, the Word of God, is a completely invisible phenomenon in its power and source, yet it requires visible means of communication, such as the mouth, the lips, and the Bible. It always results in visible fruits, moreover, for from it come repentance, love, service, dedication, and martyrdom, the life of the community. The invisible sources are never present without their visible counterparts. For Luther the visible and invisible aspects of the church are two sides of a coin. There is but one church. It has an internal and an external character, a body and a soul.[9] It is not helpful to think of these characteristics as primary and secondary, or proper and improper, or narrow and wide. This creates a false dichotomy. The visible and invisible natures of the church are descriptions of a single reality.

The church, to Luther, is neither a fairy tale nor an institution, but a community born out of the intervention of God in the world of men and manifest with the characteristics of God's work in the daily and common life of men.

This community is both human and divine, but it is clear that it exhibits all the aspects of any other community in society. It can be compared to the concept of a nation which has a "harmony of hearts found only among countrymen, felt most vividly when confronted by foreigners, a common type and a common history, a genuine spirit of brotherliness, a willingness to sacrifice for one another, a common pride, and a common love for something bigger and greater

---

8*Works of Luther* (Philadelphia: Muhlenberg Press, 1931), V, 125 ff.
9See Pauck's discussion, *op. cit.*, pp. 31 ff.

than they are."[10] It can be called a solidarity of persons. This solidarity, which includes Christ himself, is so important that every distinction of race, sex, social standing, and ecclesiastical dignity is obliterated. There is only one Christian estate even though there may be different offices. This solidarity finds its highest expression in the Sacrament of the Altar, which is the climactic experience in the life of the people of God.

The Lutheran confessions meant to capture this idea and preserve it. The Augsburg Confession simply declares the church to be this community. It confesses its faith that this community will continue forever. The form may vary. No particular structure is necessary. There is but one such community. The locus of the community is the Gospel. This confession, beautiful in its simplicity, was, however, subject to various interpretations. Interpreted it was, and quickly too, until divergent patterns cut across the original clarity.

It is our duty now to examine them.

THE INVISIBLE COMMUNITY

The first pattern of community in contemporary Lutheranism that we shall examine is that of repristination theology. This is a name commonly given to a type of Lutheran confessionalism which seeks to maintain a pure and absolute theology by the use of the scientific methods formulated by the Lutheran fathers of the late sixteenth and the seventeenth centuries. This means to its disciples, coincidentally, a revival of the perfect theology of Luther as they understand it, as perfectly expressed in the Lutheran confessions. We choose as our representative Dr. Francis Pieper, whose three-volume *Dogmatics* is the dominating influence in American Lutheran orthodoxy, especially in the Lutheran Church —Missouri Synod.[11]

10Heinrich Bornkamm, *Luther's World of Thought*, trans. Martin H. Bertram (St. Louis: Concordia Publishing House, 1958), p. 137. This is one of the more delightful excursions into Luther's ideas.
11Francis Pieper, *Christian Dogmatics*, trans. Theodore Engelder and W. W. F. Albrecht (3 vols.; St. Louis: Concordia Publishing House, 1951-53).

To this school, the Christian religion is absolute. There is no possible supplement, improvement, or development. It is unsurpassable. The basis for the absoluteness lies in its possession of two perfect criteria. First, it delivers a perfect salvation, and second, its source and norm is a perfect book, the Bible. The criterion of a perfect salvation is proved by the perfect atonement of Jesus Christ, who died vicariously for our sins. The vicarious satisfaction of the death of Christ is the absolute key to Christian theology. Any modification or supplement to this doctrine destroys the perfection of theology. Likewise, the unsurpassability of its perfection is guaranteed by the Bible whose infallibility is proved by the authority vested in it by the perfect Redeemer and by the method in which it was given, i.e., by verbal inspiration.

Similarly, Dr. Pieper envisions the church as a perfect and divine entity, an invisible communion of faith, the *coetus electorum,* that is, the assembly or communion of the elect. The church, he says, is the sum total of "all those, and only those, in whom the Holy Spirit has worked the faith. . . ."[12] The believers are the elect, that is, those "actually saved," by the initiating and predestinating grace of God, and who "without fail . . . enter life eternal."[13] The constituting factor of the church is faith. This faith is a divine gift from God and retains its divine character even when possessed by the believer. It is completely in God's control. Because this faith is divine, it is invisible and known only to God. The true church is, therefore, invisible, and any description which speaks of the church in terms of its visibility "confuses the marks of the church with the church proper."[14]

Pieper admits that the word "church" is also used to refer to the visible community which confesses the Christian faith and receives the Sacraments, but this is using the word in an improper sense, for the true church is not visible. The

12*Ibid.,* III, p. 397.
13*Ibid.,* p. 479.
14*Ibid.,* p. 409.

presence of the invisible church can be detected by the outward signs, such as the Sacraments, but its true nature must be considered divine and not human, even though the church consists of human individuals.

Indeed, in contrast to any kind of human community, the church is called a "spiritual" kingdom. Christians are in a "spiritual body, a spiritual house of living stones."[15] The church is the pious, believing Christians, but it is those Christians "assembled in the spirit." They are the church in their faith, on their divine side, as it were, and even though this spiritual membership is reflected in their human side, it is not this human manifestation which is the church itself.

This true invisible church is universal. It encompasses all those who possess faith, wherever they may be on the earth and whatever outward church, if any, may regard them as members. The church is the total number of the elect, but it is nothing more than the sum of individuals who have been grasped by the grace of God.

What creates the church? That which makes the church the church is faith, the invisible faith created by invisible grace. It is only this kind of faith which establishes membership in the church. Neither holding membership in a church body, nor the outward use of the Sacraments, nor public confession of faith, nor zeal for a moral life, nor any mystical or emotional experience apart from the possession of faith is any criterion of true church membership. Nothing but the absence of faith separates the individual from the church. Excommunication does not separate if faith is present; false doctrines held in ignorance cannot blot out grace, although they are extremely dangerous; the lack of Baptism through lack of opportunity is not absolute separation. This factor of faith is so absolute that even the relationship of the Christians to each other is of little importance. The relationship to God is all-important. The emphasis is really not upon the assembly of the elect but on the individual elected. It is not the communion of believers which is the church's true nature

---

15 *Ibid.*, p. 401 ff.

but the individual believers' faith that constitutes the church. What kind of community is it? One is tempted to say at the outset that this is really not a community at all. What kind of community can it be when it is purely supernatural and has no sociological reality? Can there be community when there are no interhuman relationships involved? We must not be too hasty with this judgment, however, for although this school maintains the absolutely invisible and divine character of the church, it also permits certain communal aspects to enter by the back door. For example, even though the true church is universal, it does have a particular aspect, the local congregation. The difference between the universal and the local church is not one of kind but only of number and locus of authority. The organized congregation is the medium of the dispensation of grace and is considered a divine institution ordained by God. Christians are required by divine mandate to form themselves into congregations, which in the most proper sense are the visible signs of the true church, if one dares to use this language at all. The church is the elect who assemble themselves into congregations.

Further, there must be safeguards of a tangible nature to this community of faith. Hedges must be built about this community. Even though only God knows the heart and thus where the church is, man can assuredly know where the church is not. Faith can be hedged about with the strong walls of pure doctrine, which help keep the faith even though they do not produce it. For example, there is no church where the vicarious satisfaction of Christ is denied. And there can be no church where the means of grace are absent or improperly understood. Any reliance upon ethical accomplishments or the merits of free will or upon any conception of faith which does not give the full credit to the Holy Spirit must, *ipso facto*, be a denial of the church.

In addition to this, certain other communal characteristics are noted. The church is one because all its members believe the same thing. There can be no variations in the essential doctrines of the faith. The unity of the church consists in the unity of belief. The church has a historical continuity, for it has preserved perfect and inviolate the apostolic doctrine, that is, the doctrine taught by the apostles. By the same token, the church is immutable. There has been no change in the communal belief in all the ages. And, certainly, the church worships. The individual elect assemble for praise and instruction.

What is the place of the individual in this community? The individual is everything. The community is the simple addition of individuals. The community is nothing more than this, it is nothing in itself. The charge of pure individualism must be qualified, however, by calling attention to certain secondary aspects again. If the individual obeys his Lord, he will love his fellow man, and not the least his Christian brother. Thus the individual is always involved in inter-human relationships, but this must be stressed as a result of the coming to faith and cannot be considered as a necessary part of the true nature of the community. A community of personal relationships results from the gift of faith, but it is not these relationships which are the community. They are after the fact.

Closely allied with this are the relationships between the church and the goal of the faith, salvation. The goal is quite simply a right relationship with God which results in eternal life. The eye is upon heaven. Heaven is a place in another world, a world which succeeds to this temporal and spatial existence. We enter heaven one by one. The church might be thought of as a means to this end, but this must be interpreted carefully. God may use the church as an instrument to carry out his plan to bring men to salvation in the next world, but this means must be considered secondary and not necessary. That is to say, it is the reception of the gift of faith which is necessary and the actual means. The church is the result of the means, but not an absolute result. This school faithfully upholds the ancient dictum that there is no salvation outside of the church, but it argues in a circle to sustain its view. Salvation is centered upon the faith of the individual. It is this faith that creates the church, which is the collection of the saved individuals. The church as community has little or no direct relationship to salvation.

THE VOLUNTARY COMMUNITY

The term pietism is often used to designate the various phenomena of separatism, legalism, asceticism, mysticism, and quietism. Sometimes pietism refers only to the early reaction against the formalistic orthodoxy of the seventeenth century. Both uses of the word are too narrow. Pietism may indeed degenerate into one or more of the "isms" mentioned, but this is neither its intent nor an accurate description of its real nature. We use the word to mean the theological position which maintains that man and his religious life are both the proper beginning of and the primary subject of theological inquiry. Whereas the age of orthodoxy had proposed that the objective side of the God-man relationship provided the only proper materials for theology, and therefore emphasized God's revelatory truth, pietism holds that the subjective side of the God-man interaction is also necessary to a full understanding of the Christian faith. Indeed, the pietists make the inner experience of the Christian their consuming interest, although they do not intend to neglect the objective character of God's acts in history. In adopting a different theological base than Lutheran orthodoxy, pietism does not consider itself any less scientific in its methodology. Quite the contrary, it claims to have a more comprehensive scientific character since it can use the empirical methods of psychology as well as the more limited historical and logical methods of strict orthodoxy.

The most influential theological spokesman for pietism in Lutheranism in this century was Ole Hallesby, former professor and dean at *Menighetsfakultetet,* The Free Theological Faculty in Oslo, Norway. He is the author of a two-volume dogmatics and numerous devotional books and commentaries for laymen.[16]

Hallesby conceives of the church as a society of God-dedicated persons which springs up among those who have had the common experience of discovering a living relationship with God. The church is like the members of a family who, having been born into a particular relationship to each other, love and serve one another out of a feeling of mutuality which is automatically a part of their inherited kinship. The church consists of individual Christians, but individuals who stand in a special relationship to one another, a relationship which must be understood as meaning more than the simple addition of individuals. A family is more than a sum of its members, even though it is the members who together make up the family.

God has a plan, says Hallesby, a plan conceived in eternity but carried out in history. The plan is to bring a rebellious mankind back under his rule, that is, into his kingdom. The goal of history is the realization of God's will on earth as it is in heaven.[17] Revelation can be described as the activity of God in history carrying out his plan. Man is the object of this activity. If God's kingdom is to be realized, it must be through the cooperation of individual men. God's will cannot be imposed upon men, for this would violate the personality he has given them. Their free decision is necessary. At the same time, men are under such a heavy load of sin and guilt that they cannot exercise their free will, at least by initiating a relationship to God. God had to find a way, says Hallesby, whereby men could freely decide to commit themselves to God and yet understand their own lack of merit. The will of God can be realized only in a context where men choose to obey God without accruing to themselves any credit for the obedience. Pietism is interested in the psy-

---

16Ole Hallesby, *Den kristelige Troslaere* (2 vols.; Kristiania: Lutherstiftelsens Forlag, 1921).
17*Ibid.*, II, 174 ff.

chological process by which men are brought to the point of this decision. Hallesby calls it the "God-experience," or rebirth.

If the individual accepts the will of God, he is given a new life. Justification is always accompanied by an actual moral transformation. The life of love invariably follows justification. The possession of love is not a condition for justification but is rather that quality exhibited by the one who has been declared justified. In the rebirth the individual receives Christ's spirit in his heart and lives from that moment on in a common life with God. It is this reborn person, this new individual, born into God's family on earth, who is a "relative" of all those who have been similarly reborn.

The church comes into being when these Christians recognize one another and decide to live together in a community of love, witness, discipline, and worship. This can be called a voluntary community because it is the will of reborn men which calls it into being. God, of course, is the ultimate source of all, but it is men who by their obedience and concern bring about the community itself in its historical manifestation.

That which makes this community what it is is the presence of "living relationships." He means by this that the relationships must be "real," or "actual." They are not formal relationships only or the indication of status, such as the state of being saved. Something actually passes from one member to the other when a "living" relationship exists. The relationship is alive and can change. It can grow, develop, recede. It must always be in action, producing, reacting, stimulating.

These relationships are thought of in two senses. First, Hallesby thinks of the relationship to God, a relationship which comes alive in the God-experience. Second, he always includes the relationship of one Christian to another, an idea which multiplies into a whole system of relationships, and therefore a community. The relationship to God may be primary, but the relationship to other Christians always follows, and it is this which creates the church. The church has two dimensions: a vertical one, the commitment to God, and a horizontal one, meaning the love relationship to other Christians.

What kind of community is created by these relationships? Six points should be stressed. First, negatively, the community is not that of a union around a common aim or ideal. Nor is it primarily born out of any kind of common agreement, such as a doctrinal agreement. Second, positively, there is an inner, organic life that binds the members together into a whole—a common life which is quite apart from the meeting of minds. How a self can be related to another self is quite indescribable. The mysterious quality of being able to unite with another person or group of persons can be experienced but not understood completely. Third, this inner oneness flows out of the common oneness of the members with Christ. Christians are like branches which have been grafted into a common stem. Neither the means of grace nor their administration makes the church the church. These presuppose a living church. The church is neither the society of the baptized nor of the called. The church possesses the life of God because the individuals in it have assumed the divine nature of God in will and purpose and share that dedication together. Fourth, the church is the body of Christ because it is obedient to his will. The communal life is one of discipleship, of obedience and discipline.

The fifth point requires more explanation. The community is always visible. Hallesby contends that the "living union, which binds the Christians together in a congregation, is of a spiritual and invisible kind but . . . always reveals itself as an outward and visible expression of the life and work together. . . ."[18] The church always appears, even to the natural eye of man, in some empirical fashion. It is a sociological institution. The fellowship which the spiritual life

---

18*Ibid.*, pp. 494 ff.

creates cannot be hid and is an infallible guide to the existence of the inner spiritual kinship. It is true, however, that the precise boundaries of the church remain somewhat undetermined, for the secrets of the heart cannot always be judged by men, but this does not undermine the essential visible reality of the community itself.

Last, the church is pure. The community must exercise vigilance in keeping its witness to the world inviolate. Two extremes must be avoided. It must not become so lax as to abandon its task of self-criticism and permit its community to deteriorate. At the same time, it must not become so critical of itself that it judges with a severity lacking in love. The Spirit of God will lead so that the community will reveal to the world its good works.

The place of the individual thus is clear. He is the foundation stone out of which the community is built. The individual comes first, but through his action a community always comes into being. The integrity of the individual is never compromised, but the resultant community is considered a necessary consequence of obedience.

The relationship between the community and salvation is clear as well. The church is a means to an end. It is the way in which God brings about the goal of history, obedience of men to his will, his kingdom. The community is a microcosm of the future perfect life in heaven. It is a plank in God's kingdom plan, as Hallesby puts it. The church is, therefore, not the same as salvation, for that is still defined strictly in terms of the God-experience, but it is the means by which the salvation is expressed. The church is thus a necessary means, for unless the living union with Christ results in a living union with other Christians, salvation is lost.

THE ESCHATOLOGICAL COMMUNITY

By Lundensian theology we mean the new approach to the Reformation which has been fostered by the Theological Faculty at the University of Lund in Sweden. This effort has been motivated by two main concerns. First, it has sought to take into account the developments in both philosophy and theology since the time of the Reformation, and second, it believes that both repristination theology and pietism misunderstand the real Luther. Luther research has been one of its most important activities. The view it presents is claimed, therefore, to be a more valid interpretation of Luther which is at the same time more biblically and philosophically sound. The movement began in the late nineteenth century and continues to grow in influence in world Lutheranism.

We have chosen two representatives for this school. Bishop Anders Nygren and Bishop Gustaf Aulén, both former members of the Lund Faculty, have written widely in the last fifty years on the doctrine of the church. The main sources for this discussion are Aulén's Dogmatics, now translated into English, and Nygren's writings for the ecumenical movement.[19]

The church, says Bishop Aulén, is "a heavenly organism, but at the same time perceptible and visible on earth, existing on the border between two worlds, two aeons, having a quality that transcends every present age in history."[20] It is "a divine creation in the world of men."[21] The intervention of God's love has brought about a new order of existence. The Lundensians prefer to call this new existence the *corpus Christi*, the body of Christ, or the *regnum Christi*, the reign of Christ. It is actually the existence of objective reality which was given in and with the incarnation of Christ and which continues to this day as his reign. The church is an eschatological entity, that is, it is the reality of Christ in the world which is between an event in the past, the finished

19Gustaf Aulén, trans. Eric Wahlstrom and G. Everett Arden, *The Faith of the Christian Church* (4th ed.; Philadelphia: Muhlenberg Press, 1948). Of special interest is Anders Nygren, trans. Alan Carlsten, *Christ and His Church* (Philadelphia: The Westminster Press, 1956) and *This Is the Church*, trans. Carl C. Rasmussen (Philadelphia: The Muhlenberg Press, 1952), which is a symposium edited by Nygren.
20Gustaf Aulén, *Church, Law, and Society* (New York: Charles Scribner's Sons, 1948), p. 16.
21Aulén, *The Faith of the Christian Church*, p. 335.

work on the cross, and an event in the future, the eschaton, the end of history.

Still other language might be helpful. The church can be called "the new age." As all men were bound in a great oneness in Adam, so now a new humanity is bound to Christ. Whereas the old age, before Christ, was one of death, Christ has brought a new age of life. This life is a dominion of power, a new order of existence. The church *is* that order. Quite in line with this idea is Paul's phrase "in Christ." To be "in Christ" is to participate in his life, that is, to have faith in him. To have faith is to be touched by the reality of Christ, which is another way of saying that to have faith is to be encompassed within the divine reality, to be enveloped in the love of God. Faith is not so much an individual matter as it is a status, a place, an order of being. Faith is standing within the realm of activity of the Spirit. It is the state of "being worked on."

The incorporation of the individual into this body comes about through Baptism. The Christian loses his independent existence and becomes a member of Christ's body, just as the branch is grafted into the vine and becomes a part of it.

That which creates this divine reality, the church, is the Gospel. This is another way of saying that it is Christ who creates the church, for he is the Gospel. Wherever the Gospel is preached, there this divine eschatological community comes into being because the power of Christ touches and transforms that into which it comes in contact. The Sacraments are a means of the Gospel or, more traditionally, of Christ himself "as he is present with us and meets us here on earth."[22] To say it in another way, the church is Christ himself, his embodiment upon earth. It is an organism which is the continuance of a people which transcends both history and thought, although it is at the same time revealed in history and is accessible both to experience and description.

Luther's simplest definition of the church, the community

22Nygren, *This Is the Church*, p. 10.

of believers, is correct, according to Aulén, but it does not convey the full meaning of Luther's own conception.[23] There is too much of the air of sociological categories which lead one astray. The social activity of likeminded believers does not bring the church into being. Any view which relates to the quality of faith or human endeavor of individuals is based upon a subjective piety which the Lundensians completely reject. Indeed, the church is never adequately defined when its definition is framed only in terms of the people. The church cannot be considered quantitatively. It is not the summation of anything—the addition of congregations or individuals or confessional organizations. The church must be understood in terms of its givenness, its thereness, its objectivity, that is, its being. And this being must be conceived as a divine reality which permeates and exists in this world. It is a structured entity which defies every rationalistic metaphysics and which cannot be defined in terms of an ordinary understanding of community.

How is this key concept, the body of Christ, to be understood? It is not a figurative or a metaphorical term but a symbol of a concrete, living reality which exists in and among men. It is the presence of Christ among his people. The church and Christ are correlative, that is, one is never without the other. To use other language, the church is the continuous work of Christ. It is a means of grace, which, again, is simply saying the means by which Christ comes. They are the self-impartation of divine love, which is God, or Christ, whichever is more convenient to say. Everything is directed back to God's activity in the world through Christ. It is Christ who constitutes the church, using certain means. It is he who makes the church what it is, who is lord and owner of the church, and, indeed, as we said, who is the church himself.

What kind of community is this? It is essentially incomprehensible. What we have just done is to view this reality

---

[23]Aulén, *Till Belysning af den Lutherske Kyrkoiden* (Uppsala: Almquist & Wiksell, 1912), p. 13.

from several angles without ever grasping its center. The innermost and deepest nature of the church cannot be discovered by any scientific analysis. Only the eye of faith can really see "what" is there, and its inner compulsion has no adequate symbol to communicate what it sees. This does not mean to the Lundensians, however, that this community is an abstract idea in contrast to a historical reality. The church is also historical. No distinction between invisible and visible, or ideal and historical, or apparent and real, is true to the nature of the church.

We know where the church is because of its marks. The preaching of the Gospel, the administration of the Sacraments, the ministry, and the essential aspects of the Christian life, such as prayer, acts of charity, and evangelism, are all sociological manifestations of its objectivity. And more important, it is a real community. The Lundensians remind us of Luther's image of the church as a loaf of bread which the great baker has made out of grains of wheat. It is in effect an absolute and necessary community, an amalgamation of the people of God into a historical entity which lives in and with the world. It reacts to and on the world about it. It has relationships with the state, is the conscience of the society in which it exists, and grows and develops with the passage of time.

This community is truly eschatological, existing on the thin edge of eternity and time, participating in both qualities of existence, wholly in both and at the same time not yet wholly a part of either. It looks forward to that time when it will become wholly manifest in God's new heaven and earth.

The place of the individual in this community is really an irrelevant question. Is there any such thing as an individual in the sense in which modern man thinks of him? In his natural state, man is enveloped in a "solidary inter-relationship of sin." He is not his own lord, and therefore not a separate, definable entity which can be thought of independent from his state of being. When the love of Christ grasps him, that sinner passes into a "solidary inter-relationship of blessing," a new state in which his lord is Christ. A man is always part of something which is larger than himself. He cannot claim an identity which separates him from a community, of either sin or salvation. The Christian is completely dependent upon the church, and the church is antecedent to him. The divine reality broke the demonic enslaving power, and the dominion of Christ replaces it. Forgiveness is the means by which this becomes possible and becomes, therefore, the basis of the individual Christian life. Only in that moment of transference from the one kingdom to the other is the role of the individual in any way distinct. In the act of the recognition of forgiveness a man stands alone. At all other times he realizes his freedom and is that creature God meant him to be in the order of existence called the church.

The church is, therefore, equated with salvation. To be saved is to be in Christ, which is to be in the church. This is what salvation is, to "live under him in his kingdom," and this is what the church is.

THE DYNAMIC COMMUNITY

The neo-confessionalist school in contemporary Lutheranism is a movement which began in the time of the German church struggle under National Socialism. It is dedicated to three basic aims: (1) the restoration of Lutheranism to its true confessional understanding by a re-examination of the confessions; (2) the promotion of Lutheran participation in the ecumenical movement, thus fulfilling one of the missions of the church; (3) the communication of the Gospel in the twentieth century, with its peculiar problems. These men have no intention of repristinating the seventeenth century theology, nor do they have romanticist leanings. On the other hand, they have no pique against the century as, for example, most pietists do. They rather seek a new interpretation of what the confessions mean in order better to meet the challenges which confront the church today. They realize that the confessions have not always been interpreted properly and have often been grossly misunderstood. In any case, the new situation calls for a new emphasis. The advent of biblical criticism makes the old orthodoxy impossible. The mounting crescendo of new theological ideas, many of which are good, must be assessed and related to the Lutheran understanding of the Gospel.

This neo-confessionalism has many emphases which are similar to the Lundensian ideas. They share ecumenical interests and accept the same dynamic understanding of revelation. The neo-confessionalists, however, have greater interest in the confessions than in Luther research and are less philosophically oriented. They are inclined to be more sympathetic to both repristination and pietist theology, which the Lundensians usually reject summarily. In fact, the neo-confessionalists might be described as "mediating theologians" to the extent that they seek to ameliorate the tensions between these two schools and to provide a new way in Lutheran theology which would embody the concerns of these traditional approaches.

We choose as our representative Dr. Edmund Schlink, professor at the University of Heidelberg and author of *The Theology of the Lutheran Confessions* and numerous contributions in ecumenical publications.[24]

What is the church? Schlink maintains that the definition in the Augsburg Confession is correct and sufficient.[25] The church is the community of believers in which the Gospel is preached and the Sacraments administered. Two important things are said. First, the church is a community. It is the fellowship of believers. This is what it is. The development of a deeper or more philosophical ontology, such as in the

---

24Edmund Schlink, *Theologie der Lutherischen Bekenntnisschriften* (München: Chr. Kaiser Verlag, 1948). The clearest summary of his thought occurs in his article "The Lutheran Churches," found in *The Nature of the Church*, ed. R. Newton Flew (London: SCM Press, 1952).
25Schlink, *Theologie der Lutherischen Bekenntnisschriften*, p. 269.

Lundensian school, is unnecessary and even dangerous. But of very great importance is the second aspect. This community is determined by what happens in it. The church is constituted by "event." One can even say that the church is "event."[26]

Schlink means by "event" that the church is dynamic in character. It is brought into being by the preaching of the Gospel, not by the possession of the Gospel, but by the actual verbal proclamation. A second form of the Gospel, the Sacraments, is also necessary, and they must actually be administered. It is the actual distribution and reception of the Sacraments that makes the church, not correct theology or again simple possession of the rites. The relative clause of the Augsburg Confession's definition is thus the main emphasis. The church is where something happens. Indeed, it is the "happening" itself. It is a dynamic community.

The church is a community where God is acting—not only where he has acted in the past, but where he is acting now. And where God is acting, we know that there is response from man. God's action and man's response cannot be separated. They are part of one action. One cannot have either a completely objective or a completely subjective theology. Theology is always paradoxical, for theology is the communication and interpretation of God's actions, and this always involves man. Since God is what he is, the unfathomable being whose accessibility to man is limited, and man is what he is, a finite, sinful creature, the relationship between the two always introduces unsolvable problems, at least logically unsolvable. Schlink maintains that theology is therefore dialectical by nature.[27] Both orthodoxy and pietism have points to emphasize. Both are wrong in claiming the whole truth.

The church "happens" at that point of contact between God and man. And that which happens is a continuing com-

---

26Schlink, "The Lutheran Churches," *op. cit.*, p. 61.
27The presuppositions for Schlink's dialectical theology are outlined in his article "Weisheit und Torheit," *Kerygma and Dogma*, I, No. 1 (1955), 1-22.

munity. The church is the believers who share with one
another the fellowship of the Gospel, those who have responded in faith to the call and by it have been brought to
a new life. The community thus created is defined in terms
of both faith and love, in terms of not only a receiving but
a doing, a fruit-bearing of faith. The reality of the church
does not allow the separation of justification and sanctification in the sense that justification only be considered necessary to the church.

What creates the church? It is this one action which has
two aspects. God acts, using the church as his instrument in
the preaching of the Gospel and the gift of the Sacraments.
Man responds, not only in repentance and faith to God, but
in the exercise of love to his fellow believers and fellow men.
The receiving of God's grace and the doing of it create the
community.

What kind of community is it? It is a real, visible, sociological community of interpersonal relationships. The members participate. They share a common grace and common
burdens. This giving of self to each other and working for
one another in love can never be separated from the common
hearing of the Gospel, through which the Holy Spirit sends
love and faith, which, in turn, unite the believers in one love.
The church is divine, because God is involved, and it is
human, because men are involved. It is both. This is its
unique character.

This community is both local and universal. All believers
share in the life of this community. It is all Christendom.
The local congregation is the church too, but it cannot be
isolated from the wholeness of the church, either in faith or
in any geographical limitation. Doctrine cannot divide the
church, for even where there is the slightest glimmer of the
Gospel, there the church happens. The church is both an institution, sociologically verifiable and analyzable, and an
invisible spiritual fellowship which can be seen only with
the eyes of faith. It is historical and moves, changes, and

develops with history, reflecting the intellectual and cultural prejudice of its own age. It is not merely a transcendent possibility on the other side of time. But it is also an external creation of God which shall continue to exist forever. It has both diversity and unity, is both holy and sinful, without any necessary form and yet always existing in a particular form, confessing to the truth of the Gospel, yet always critical of and willing to reinterpret the Gospel.

What is the place of the individual in this community? He is both before and after it. It is through the Gospel acting in the community that the individual is brought to faith. The community is therefore before the act of faith. But at the same time it is into the community that the believer is brought. It exists after him. It is by the act of faith that the community is created, for it is response of men which makes the church a community. It may be true that it is impossible to conceive of the individual as an absolutely independent entity. He cannot be divorced completely from a community of either sin or salvation, but at the same time it is in the community of blessing that he becomes an individual. He becomes the creature God meant him to be. The church gives him the gift of freedom, and this is the prime aspect of individuality. The individual and the community are therefore put into a paradox. Neither can do without the other, and the full integrity of each is maintained. Pure individualism is an insult to the Gospel, but absolute community dismisses the real aim of God's action, to make men into the creatures God meant them to be.

And what of the relationship between the church and salvation? The dialectical approach is used again. The church is both the means and the end of salvation. To bring men into his community is what God aims to do. It, therefore, is salvation. But at the same time it is only a means to salvation, for the end is not yet. Schlink likes to characterize the church as the pilgrim people. They look forward to consummation of God's purpose at some future time and yet at the same time enjoy the fruits of that victory now.[28] A Christian is always on his way to salvation, while at the same time he is saved. Similarly, the church is that community in which the sinner is being saved, while at the same time it is the end of his salvation, for God has no greater gift for him now than the faith and love of this fellowship. Therefore the church can never be simply equated with salvation, but neither can it ever be divorced from it.

PATTERNS OF COMMUNITY

We have illustrated four patterns of community in contemporary Lutheran ecclesiology. The first, that of repristination theology, conceives of the church as a divine, invisible community. The community is nothing more than the collection of the elect individuals. This emphasis is so strong that it is a virtual denial of community, at least in any sociological sense, and thus of the meaning of the Reformation. The second, the view of pietism, has a genuine communal concept in that it emphasizes the visible, interhuman relationships as the constituting factor of the nature of the church. The community, however, is a secondary emphasis, even though a necessary one, because the primary concern is for the God-experience of the individual. The third view documented, issuing from the Lundensian school, is an understanding of the church which posits absolute and necessary community. This community is eschatological, having a quality of existence different from that of ordinary historical realities, and yet exhibits all the sociological aspects of community life. The interpretation of the contemporary neo-confessionalists, the fourth position, describes the church as a community of polarities. Both human and divine, both historical and other-worldly, both objective and subjective, the church is conceived in terms of that which creates it, the

28Schlink discussed the eschatological significance of the church in his address to the Second Assembly of the World Council of Churches found in *The Evanston Report*, ed. W. A. Visser 't Hooft (New York: Harper & Bros., 1954).

action of God and the response of man. Both the individual and the community are held to be necessary.

The over-all pattern, therefore, moves from nearly pure individualism to nearly absolute communal emphasis, with two variations in between, one which begins with the individual and ends up with community and the other placing the individual and community in a dialectical relationship.

We have not assumed the task of criticizing the patterns in terms of their biblical validity. However, it seems evident that their relationship to original Lutheranism can be characterized. The repristination school and pietism have over-emphasized particular aspects of Luther's view, to the exclusion of other aspects. The repristination school has been the more guilty of the two, denying a very important part of Luther's thought, namely, the sociological reality of the church. The Lundensian school has introduced a new dimension to the Lutheran view, bringing to light a side of the Reformation never before emphasized in this way. Lutherans will have to decide if this emphasis captures the essential meaning of original Lutheranism. The neo-confessionalists have, to this writer's view, represented more clearly and fully the Reformation concept.

In any case, the clear conclusion is that if contemporary Lutheranism wishes to continue the Reformation emphasis upon the church as a real community, it must reopen the question of the nature of the church in a more radical way than it has so far displayed any willingness to do.

III

Unity and Diversity in the New Testament

JAMES H. BURTNESS

After five days of Religious Emphasis Week on a midwestern campus, a sorority housemother summed up the situation by saying to one of the speakers, "It's all so inspiring. And each one of us has to worship his own god in his own way. That's right, isn't it?" The same sentiment was expressed in another way by a girl who came up to a professor in the lunchroom and commented, "Well, I see you're on a religion kick this week." At noon luncheons, dormitory discussions, evening meetings, and class lectures, students and faculty listened to a barrage of religious comment from a Jewish rabbi, a Roman Catholic priest, and Methodist, Presbyterian, Unitarian, Lutheran, and Baptist ministers. One speaker, with unconcealed delight, told about his fourteen-year-old boy who had successively been a Methodist, a Jew, a Unitarian, and who was now a "very healthy" agnostic. The final word in every discussion was: "You have your opinion and I have mine." That closed the argument because, of course, everyone knows that religion is a matter of opinion.

This attitude accounts for the fact that religion has always provided ready material for undergraduate bull sessions. One cannot very well argue about the dates of the Napoleonic Wars, or the molecular structure of benzene, or the debt of

DR. BURTNESS is assistant professor of systematic theology at Luther Theological Seminary, St. Paul, Minn.

62

the United Nations, or the distance to the moon. That is, one cannot argue about such things without being sufficiently well informed to be able to evaluate the subtleties involved in the interpretation of the data. If one has not made an independent study of such matters, the only thing to do is to go to an authoritative source and "get the answer." After all, facts are facts. But religion is different. Religion is a matter of opinion.

One finds this attitude even in seminary classrooms. The theological student who is exposed to the bewildering complexity of diverse interpretations of Christianity, or of the Bible, or of a particular book in the Bible, or even a passage or a word, often feels that he is simply not equipped to argue with the experts. And since the experts don't agree among themselves, the solution lies in not taking any of them very seriously. For every opinion that can be quoted on one side of an issue, there is one that can be quoted on the other side. Thus theology becomes a very fascinating game in which one tracks down, like a latter-day Sherlock Holmes, quotations from various authorities with which to impress one's professors and fellow students. But throughout the process it is clear that none of this is really very important. The theological student ought not to get too wrapped up in these opinions. When he becomes a pastor the important thing will be to get down to the business of raising the budget, building the parish education unit, and organizing the interest groups.

Now there is an element of truth in this kind of talk. There is no question but that a man must ultimately make up his own mind about whether he is going to worship God and, if so, to what religious group he wishes to belong. But at this point a very important distinction must be made. The fact that each man may decide to accept or reject the claim of a particular religion does not mean that his evaluation of the content of that claim is necessarily valid.

If someone were to say, for instance, "The Constitution

of the United States says that everyone should eat plenty of cottage cheese," or "The Charter of the United Nations tells us that all human babies have a secret desire to be turtles," the reply ought not to be, "Well, that's a very interesting opinion." The reply ought to be, "It doesn't say that at all!" In the case of Christianity also there are historical documents of the primitive Christian community which are taken to be authoritative in one way or another by all Christians. The interpretation of these documents is not a purely arbitrary affair, not simply a matter of opinion. There is the task of establishing the text with which one is going to work. There is the problem of translation. The historical situation in which the document was written must be taken into account. There are principles of interpretation. There are critical tools of historical research. Opinion is a factor in any statement about anything. But in the interpretation of the New Testament it is a much smaller factor than is generally acknowledged.

There is no such thing as a purely objective knowledge of bare facts. The knower is always involved in the knowing. All knowledge consists of some combination of fact and interpretation. This is as true of scientific knowledge as it is of religious knowledge, though it must be granted that the interpretation component is not as large in the former as in the latter. To say that religion is a matter of opinion is thus an unfortunate choice of terminology, especially in relation to Christianity with its strong commitment to the collection of documents in the Bible. Every interpreter has his presuppositions, and there must be the recognition of the need for diversity in theological expression. But this diverse expression must be carried out within certain limits and interpretations arrived at with the use of certain tools. In the New Testament we do not get the impression at all that religion is a matter of opinion. We are impressed rather with the fact that there is one message, but that this one message is expressed in a number of different ways.

DIVERSITY OF EXPRESSION

The early dogmatic theologies of the Reformation era were written assuming the unity of the biblical message. This does not necessarily mean that there was no recognition whatever of the fact that the various authors of the biblical documents express themselves in different ways. But there was no stress on these differences. The Bible was the Word of God, and God does not speak out of both sides of his mouth. Thus a verse from Proverbs may be listed along with a verse from Romans with no indication of the divergent sources.

One of the most important of these early works was Melanchthon's *Loci Communes,* which helped set the pattern for future dogmatic constructions during the period of orthodoxy in the seventeenth century. It consists of theological comment on a number of places (loci), or topics, which were assembled on the basis of Melanchthon's study of Romans. Passages from all over the Bible are quoted in support of each comment. The interesting thing is that there is no embarrassment whatever about pouring all the other biblical writers into this Pauline framework.

The recognition of diversity in the New Testament writers came in the nineteenth century along with a general interest in the historical character of the Christian faith and a specific interest in the humanity of Jesus, and consequently in the humanity of the New Testament writers.[1] The mood of the period is obvious in *The Theology of the New Testament* by G. B. Stevens, a standard work for a generation of theological students in American seminaries during the early part of this century. The book is divided into: "The Teaching of Jesus According to the Synoptic Gospels," "The Teaching of Jesus According to the Fourth Gospel," "The Primitive Apostolic Teaching," "The Theology of Paul," "The Theology of the Epistle to the Hebrews," "The Theology of the

---

[1] It was specifically against this emphasis that Karl Barth shouted out that "God is in heaven, and you are on earth" in his 1921 edition of *The Epistle to the Romans.* In his 1956 essay, "The Humanity of God," Barth modifies his early position and takes a more positive attitude toward the historical emphases of liberal theology.

Apocalypse," "The Theology of John." Another example is *The Varieties of New Testament Religion* by E. F. Scott. In each case the New Testament is taken to be a collection of diverse theologies, with no embarrassment concerning the absence of any unity.

Now, if it is necessary for us to go through, rather than around, the period of orthodoxy in the seventeenth century, it is also necessary for us to go through, rather than around, the period of liberalism in the nineteenth century. If it is important to acknowledge the unity of the New Testament message, it is also important to recognize the diversity of expression in the proclamation of this message. This is not simply to point out seemingly contradictory notions, such as Paul's "a man is not justified by works of the law but through faith" (Gal. 2:16) and James' "a man is justified by works and not by faith alone" (James 2:24), or of the positive attitude toward the state in Romans (13:1-7) and the negative attitude toward the state in Revelation (13:1-18). The recognition of diversity among the New Testament writers leads one into a greater appreciation of the language and basic motifs and emphases of each individual author.

The fundamental motif, for instance, in the Gospel according to Mark (and consequently also in the Gospels according to Matthew and Luke) is the kingdom of God. Mark sums up the preaching of Jesus with the words: "The time is fulfilled, and the kingdom of God is at hand; repent, and believe in the gospel" (1:15). In the Markan account Jesus says, "With what can we compare the kingdom of God, or what parable shall we use for it?" (4:30). For Mark the parables are pictures of the kingdom of God. The miracle stories are pictures of the kingdom, too, but they are acted-out pictures. Through both the parables and the miracles Jesus is proclaiming the kingdom of God.[2] There is a great deal of room for discussion on the subtleties of the meaning

---

2Cf. Alan Richardson, *The Miracle Stories of the Gospel* (London: SCM, 1941) and James Kallas, *The Significance of the Synoptic Miracles* (Greenwich, Connecticut: Seabury, 1961).

of this phrase. Does Jesus announce that the kingdom of God is going to come in the future, or does he actually usher it in? Or is it possible to speak of the kingdom as both realized and future?[3] Can the kingly rule of God be identified with the lordship of Jesus, or must these two be carefully distinguished though never completely separated?[4] These are areas where questions of interpretation are legitimate and necessary. But if there is a failure to recognize the centrality of the kingdom of God motif in Mark's gospel, it is very likely that there will also be a failure to understand Mark's use of the sayings of Jesus, the parables, the miracle stories, and also the structure and progression of the narrative as a whole. Mark's way of expressing his witness to Christ is through the use of the concept of the kingdom of God.

In the Fourth Gospel an entirely different mood prevails. John does not focus on the kingdom of God. Nor does he set his witness essentially in the context of sin and salvation. That is, these are not the expressions which John uses. The words "repentance" and "forgiveness" never occur in the Fourth Gospel. The reader soon notices also that Jesus himself speaks differently in John's Gospel than he does in that of Mark. Instead of short, terse sayings, he speaks in longer discourses. The language is more symbolic than it is parabolic. The miracle stories are not explained as pictures of the kingdom. They are rather signs pointing to Jesus himself. John states the purpose of his Gospel specifically: "Now Jesus did many other signs in the presence of the disciples, which are not written in this book; but these are written that you may believe that Jesus is the Christ, the Son of God, and that believing you may have life in his name" (John 20:30, 31). The wedding at Cana is described as the "first of his signs" (2:11). And the material is arranged in

---

[3]For an introduction to some of the issues at stake in this question, cf. W. G. Kümmel, *Promise and Fulfillment* (London: SCM Press, 1957). Kümmel insists on a "now . . . but not yet" eschatology, but discusses his position in the context of the current literature on the subject.

[4]Cf. Oscar Cullmann, "The Kingship of Christ and the Church in the New Testament," *The Early Church*, ed. A. J. B. Higgins and trans. A. J. B. Higgins and Stanley Godman (London: SCM, 1956).

such a way that a miracle is usually accompanied by a discourse pointing to its significance. When Jesus feeds the multitude, he also tells them that this is not just a free lunch (6:1-14). It is a sign pointing to Jesus as the bread of life (6:35). The healing of the man born blind (9:1-41) is a sign pointing to Jesus as the light of the world (8:12). The raising of Lazarus from the dead (11:1-44) is a sign pointing to Jesus as the resurrection and the life (11:25). Not the kingdom of God, but Jesus Christ as light and life and love, is the dominant note in the Fourth Gospel.

Although the concept of the kingdom is present in the Pauline epistles, and the words life, love, and light occur, these do not constitute for Paul the focal point of his witness. Because of the large amount of material which he produced and the great variety of situations to which he wrote, Paul does not lend himself to categorization as easily as do Mark and John. There have consequently been a number of interpretations of the *paulinum centrum*.

Luther found assurance of the grace of God in the reading of Romans. Thus justification by grace through faith became for him the focal point of the Pauline witness. It is possible to put forth a strong argument for this position. However, it is very interesting that the word "justification" does not play the role in the other Pauline epistles that it does in Romans and Galatians. In the modern period there have been those who reject justification as the key to the Pauline epistles, and who find the dominant motif elsewhere. Deissmann, for instance, concludes that the real center of the Pauline witness is the phrase "in Christ."[5] C. A. Anderson Scott, in his important work on Paul *(Christianity According to St. Paul)* finds it in the word "salvation."[6] Bultmann finds it in the transition from "man prior to the revelation

---

5Adolf Deissmann, *Paul: A Study in Social and Religious History*, trans. William E. Wilson (New York: Harpers, 1912).
6Cf. also A. M. Hunter, *Interpreting Paul's Gospel* (Philadelphia: Westminster, 1954). "To unlock the words of Paul's theology, I have unashamedly borrowed the key [the word 'salvation'] which Anderson Scott, a quarter of a century ago, so successfully employed in his *Christianity According to St. Paul*, in many ways still the best book on Paul's theology we have" (p. 9).

of faith" to "man under faith."[7] To point to these various interpretations is not to say that the understanding of Paul is simply a matter of opinion. These interpretations are based on careful research and must be examined as live alternatives. It is rather to point to the fact that to get at the essential genius of Paul's witness is not an obvious or an easy task.

At any rate, Paul is not John, and John is not Mark. And there are Peter and James and the author of Hebrews, and the author of Revelation. Each writer must be read as a man with his own personality and his own peculiar way of bearing witness to Jesus Christ. To fail to recognize the humanity of the New Testament writers is to rob ourselves of the rich diversity of expression in the New Testament witness to Christ.

THE UNITY OF THE NEW TESTAMENT

It is not possible to go back to the older dogmatic use of the New Testament which supported its doctrinal statements with the almost indiscriminate use of Bible verses, quoted with little or no regard to the peculiar theological emphases of the authors of the statements. Nor would it be helpful to do so if it were possible. We can be thankful that the liberal scholars of the nineteenth century pointed out to us the humanity of the New Testament writers and the diversity of expression in their witness to Christ.

On the other hand, neither is it necessary for us to stop with the nineteenth century. The eventual sterility of this approach to the New Testament became clear with the publication of two remarkable works on the New Testament during the first decades of this century. Karl Barth's *The Epistle to the Romans* (2nd ed., 1921) did not reject the literal and historical exegesis of the nineteenth century, but it called for a recognition of the need for theological exegesis. Im-

---

[7]Rudolf Bultmann, *Theology of the New Testament*, trans. Kendrick Grobel (New York: Scribner's, 1951).

portant as is the task of careful textual and lexical and syntactical studies, the interpreter has not finished his task when he has completed this spade work. The Word must come through the words. The unity of the message must be made clear through the diversity of the expressions. Albert Schweitzer's *The Quest of the Historical Jesus* called for a recognition of the "thorough-going eschatology" in the synoptic narrative, and led the way toward the current emphasis on the acts of God[8] as the unifying note in the New Testament documents.

If E. F. Scott's *The Varieties of New Testament Religion* characterized the last generation's recognition of the diversity of expression in the New Testament, H. H. Rowley's *The Unity of the Bible* (1953) may be taken as characterizing the present recognition of the unity of the message. But the unity which is currently emphasized is not the older dogmatic unity of the seventeenth century. It is a unity which is informed by the insights of nineteenth century liberalism. Rowley begins his book with a chapter entitled "Unity in Diversity," and immediately sets out to indicate his relation to recent scholarship.

> When the writer began his theological studies it would have seemed a hazardous thing to announce a course of lectures on the Unity of the Bible. The emphasis then was predominantly on the diversity of the Bible, and such a title as that of the present work would have involved some suspicion that the author was an out-of-date obscurantist. . . . During the years of the writer's working life a very considerable change of climate has come over Biblical studies. . . . It must be said at the outset that we owe an immense debt to the scholars of those earlier days. There is diversity in the Bible, and with all the emphasis on the unity of the Bible which will be found in the present work, the diversity in which that unity is found must not be forgotten. . . . It is unnecessary to close our eyes

---

8Cf. G. E. Wright and R. H. Fuller, *The Book of the Acts of God* (Garden City: Doubleday, 1957).

to the diversity in order to insist on the unity, or to close our eyes to the unity in order to insist on the diversity.[9]

The problem, then, in the contemporary reading of the New Testament is how to state the unity while at the same time recognizing the diversity. The word which best sums up the current efforts in this direction is the word *kerygma*, which means "proclamation" or "message." One can see the root of this kerygmatic theology in Barth's call for a theological exegesis and in Schweitzer's call for thoroughgoing eschatology. "A proclamation of the facts of the death and resurrection of Christ in an eschatological setting which gives significance to the facts,"[10] is C. H. Dodd's definition of the Pauline kerygma, but it will serve as a working definition for the kerygma of the New Testament as a whole. The kerygma has to do not only with the words, but with the Word. It is proclamation of the Word of God which comes through the words of men. It does not seek to tell who God is but rather what he has done and will do. The events which reveal his gracious activity toward us are not mere facts, but facts interpreted and illuminated by the eschatological framework in which they are set. In Jesus Christ the end has come; God's promise to his people has been fulfilled.

Whereas the older dogmatic theology laid out the unity of the New Testament by setting down categories from Paul's letter to the Romans, and then forcing the other New Testament writers into this Pauline mold, the kerygmatic theology attempts to describe the unified proclamation of the New Testament in such a way that the individuality of the various New Testament witnesses can be retained. The kerygma does not characterize the message of any one New Testament writer. It is that which is common to all of them.

The synoptic motif of the kingdom of God, then, is illuminated rather than lost by the recognition of the kerygma. The kingdom of God is an eschatological motif. It is the ful-

9H. H. Rowley, *The Unity of the Bible* (London: The Carey Kingsgate Press, 1953), pp. 1-3.
10C. H. Dodd, *The Apostolic Preaching and Its Development* (London: Harper, 1936), p. 13.

fillment of the longing of the people of God for his coming
rule. Yet its consummation remains in the future. The parables are kerygmatic pictures. The miracles are kerygmatic
acts. The kingdom of God is thus one way in which the
kerygma is expressed.

John's witness is no less kerygmatic. It is simply not true
that John is concerned only with eternal ideas. In fact, John's
whole Gospel is informed by a passionate earthiness, an insistence that "the Word became flesh" (John 1:14). The
sacramental allusions that John weaves into the fabric of
the narrative serve to corroborate this conclusion. The
eschatological framework in which this Johannine kerygma
is set is a more realized eschatology than that of the Synoptic
Gospels, but it is no less decisive.

> It must be emphasized here that, rich as is the special
> contribution which John brought into the storehouse of
> Christian theology, the whole is subordinated to the un-
> escapable framework of eschatology which has always
> dominated Christian thought from the days of Jesus and
> the preaching of the apostles. The eschatological element
> in the fourth gospel is not accidental; it is fundamental.
> To have abandoned it would have been to abandon the
> biblical framework of primitive Christianity, and to run
> all the risks to which a purely metaphysical Christianity,
> divorced from history, is exposed.[11]

And Paul also is easier to understand in the light of the
kerygma. Whether one thinks of the central thrust of Paul's
writings as justification, or as Christ-mysticism, or salvation, or the transition from nonfaith to faith, it is true
throughout that Paul's primary concern is with the "facts of
the death and resurrection of Christ in an eschatological setting which gives significance to the facts."[12]

To be sure, there is obvious diversity of expression in the
writings of Mark, John, and Paul, and also James, Peter, and
the authors of Hebrews and Revelation. But within this di-

11C. K. Barrett, *The Gospel According to St. John* (London: S.P.C.K., 1955), p. 58.
12Dodd, *loc. cit.*

versity of expression there is a unity of message, a kerygmatic unity. According to the New Testament, religion is not simply a matter of opinion. It is a matter of proclaiming the saving acts of God culminating in the death and resurrection of Jesus Christ. Because God has chosen to allow this message to be proclaimed through human instruments, there is rich diversity in the expression of the message. If we are going to be faithful to the New Testament documents, we must not lose either this unity or this diversity.

MEMBERS OF THE BODY OF CHRIST

Important as are the theological formulae with which the various New Testament writers express the kerygma, it is essential that the kerygma not be reduced to a merely verbal schematization. The necessity of recognizing the fact-plus-interpretation character of the content of the New Testament has been stated. But it also must be stated that this verbal content can never be divorced from the community which was called into being by Jesus, which proclaimed the message about him, and which produced the New Testament documents to which the Christian community has continually looked for its primary witness to Christ.

Jesus himself, as far as we know, left no writings for his followers to duplicate and circulate. It is clear from a quick comparison of the language of Jesus in John and in the Synoptic Gospels that Jesus did not insist on the memorization and repetition of his exact words as the rabbis did with their disciples. What he did do was to call a group of twelve men to follow him. This event can only be understood eschatologically, for these twelve men were called to be the nucleus of the people of the new covenant, as the twelve sons of Jacob had been the nucleus of the people of the old covenant. Proclamation and community are inseparable. The church is the people of God called out by the proclamation of the message about Jesus Christ. Thus the unity and the diversity in the content of the New Testament documents have their origin in the unity and the diversity of the community out of which the documents came.

This is nowhere more clearly stated than in Paul's first letter to Corinth. When confronted by a report that there is quarreling in the congregation (1:11), Paul lets them know that their unity is to be found only in Christ (2:2). This fact releases Paul from the necessity of forcing a false unity in externals. When he deals with the marriage problems brought up in the written request for help (7:1), he avoids saying either that all must be married or that all must not be married. He rather lays out the context in which each can come to a responsible decision for himself. The same is true in his handling of the problems of food offered to idols (8:1-13) and of spiritual gifts (12:1—14:40).

Paul's orientation throughout is unity within diversity. "Now there are varieties of gifts, but the same Spirit; and there are varieties of service, but the same Lord; and there are varieties of working, but it is the same God who inspires them all in every one" (12:4-6). The body has many members, but it is only one body. The body is not an eye, or an ear, or a nose, or a hand, or a foot. It is a body in which each member contributes its own function to the life of the whole. The diverse manifestations of the Spirit are not for the benefit of the individual, but are "for the common good" (12:7). Although it is necessary to recognize the importance of each member, and not to violate or disparage his individuality, it is also necessary that each member take seriously the importance of building up the body. "Let all things be done for edification" (14:26). " 'All things are lawful,' but not all things build up" (10:23). Paul is extremely flexible as he seeks to adjust himself to the peculiar characteristics of the person with whom he is dealing. He is able to be "all things to all men" (9:22). But this flexibility is always controlled by his passion to build up the body, to "by all means save some" (9:22).

The genuineness with which Paul accepts others radically

different from himself as members of the body is evidence of his thorough commitment to the unity of the church within diversity of expression. "Now you are the body of Christ and individually members of it" (12:27). It is apparent from this letter that the congregation at Corinth was made up of some very questionable characters. Every kind of doctrinal and ethical aberration seems to be represented. Paul does not pass these off by saying, "It's all a matter of opinion." He speaks very sharply to them (1:10-15; 5:1-2; 6:7-8; 11:33; 14:18, 19; 14:36; 15:12). Yet this is not in order to make them conform to a pattern. It is rather to encourage them to function as individual members of the body. Paul does not hesitate to address them as "the church of God . . . sanctified in Christ Jesus . . . saints." (1:2. The phrase "called to be saints" would be better translated "to the called saints.") They are not asked to become something which they are not. The imperatives follow an indicative. They are to become what they *are*, members of the body.

Throughout Protestantism there is always the temptation to try to make of Christianity a purely individualistic affair. There is always the danger of losing the unity of the church because of an incorrect notion of the function of diversity. Paul insists throughout his first letter to Corinth that Christianity is not just a matter of opinion. Nor is it an every-man-for-himself affair. The diversity of the members must be respected. But the purpose of diversity is specifically that the body as a whole may function properly.

IV

The New Birth

ROY A. HARRISVILLE

"Birth from above," "new birth," "renewal," and "regeneration" are expressions common to baroque pulpit and revival tent. They are a part of the so-called "Christian vocabulary." And for some, for whom the presence or absence of these phrases in sermon or liturgy yields the criterion of a true, evangelical faith, they are the most significant part of that vocabulary. The revivalist summons his audience to the desired action with the appeal: "You must be born again!" And on Easter eve in the liturgical communions of Christendom the officiant intones: "O God, who didst enlighten this most holy night with the glory of the Lord's Resurrection: Preserve in all thy people the spirit of adoption which thou hast given, so that renewed in body and soul they may perform unto thee a pure service. . . ." Despite the use and overuse to which such expressions are put, however, often as not they are misunderstood or are totally without meaning, except as they contribute to that general religious "mood" which pervades Gothic sanctuaries or revival stadiums. For that reason, this essay will attempt an answer to the question: What do such expressions mean? That is, apart from whatever mood they may communicate, what aspect of Christian faith or life are they intended to reveal or to describe?

DR. HARRISVILLE is associate professor of New Testament at Luther Theological Seminary, St. Paul, Minn.

MODERN ANSWERS

Among the myriad uses and interpretations, at least two have gained prominence. According to the first interpretation, the "new birth" constitutes an advance in observable piety. In other words, when a man becomes a believer, he embarks on a constant journey toward perfection. With the help of God, he becomes better and better until at last, by virtue of his goodness, he enters heaven. The classical exposition of this conception of the new birth is to be found in the writings of the patron of modern Roman Catholicism, Thomas Aquinas. According to Thomas, sanctifying grace, in addition to moving the soul to conversion, bestows a *habitus*, i.e., a permanent, psychological quality in the soul. Thomas writes:

> . . . grace is a splendor of soul producing a divine love. But splendor of soul is a kind of quality, just as beauty of body. So grace is a kind of quality. . . . God's gracious will aids man in two ways: First, by stirring his soul to know, to will or to do a thing. And to this extent, that gracious effect in man is not a quality but rather a certain impulse of soul. . . . Secondly, God's gracious will aids man by infusing his soul with a certain gift of disposition *(habituale donum)*. . . . . . therefore, he infuses those whom he leads to choose the supernatural and eternal good with certain supernatural forms or qualities by which he moves them willingly and readily to choose the eternal good. And to this extent the gift of grace is a kind of quality.[1]

This *habitus* or quality of soul then expresses itself in the virtues, which Thomas describes in good Aristotelian fashion as taking their definition from their objects. Hence, whether their object is God (as in the theological virtues) or the "properly human way of life" (as in the cardinal virtues), they are capable of being "measured." For example, the degree to which one avoids the pitfall of Sabellianism on

---

[1] S. Thomae Aquinatis, *Summa Theologiae*, Cura et Studio Sac. Petri Caramello (Romae: Marietti, 1950), Prima Secundae, Quaestio CX, Articulus 2, pp. 541-542. (Trans. mine.—R. A. H.)

the one hand and that of Arianism on the other yields the criterion for "measuring" the robustness of the theological virtue of faith.[2] This concept of the new birth as expressed in reckonable behavior clearly underlies all of Thomas' ethic. It is not merely Aquinas, however, who construes the new birth in terms of an empirical and thus measurable advance. Such a volume as Karl Holl's *Luther*[3] leaves the reader with the distinct impression that despite his rejection of the Thomistic-scholastic idea of the *habitus* with its attendant signs, behind his interpretation of Luther lurks a concept of renewal construed in terms of observable piety. Of late, scholars have asserted that with all of Holl's emphasis upon the simultaneity of justification and renewal (in opposition to the "Melanchthonian," forensic view), his characterization of Luther's doctrine of justification as "the basis for a new life" or as an "analytic" (i.e., proleptic) judgment whose end or purpose is a being-made-righteous *(Gerechtmachung)*, contains in it the seeds of an idealism according to which the new life consists in a gradual and observable process of growth.[4]

The second most popular conception of the new birth has long been associated with Philip Melanchthon and Lutheran orthodoxy. This view, for which the idea of demonstrable, reckonable piety smacks of a heaven-storming idealism, has its locale in a concept of justification construed after the analogy of the courtroom, i.e., as a heavenly event *(justificatio in foro coeli)* in which God "declares" or "pronounces" the sinner righteous. The new birth, then, does not consist in a *habitus* (Thomas) or a "real righteousness" (Holl), but, as the supporters of this view are wont to put it, in a "change of status." In recent years, Werner Elert has been one of the most eloquent defenders of this view:

2*St. Thomas Aquinas, Theological Texts*, selected and translated by Thomas Gilby (London: Oxford University Press, 1955), p. 183.
3Karl Holl, *Luther, Gesammelte Aufsätze zur Kirchengeschichte* (Tübingen: J. C. B. Mohr, 1932), I, 111 ff.
4*Ibid.*, pp. 119, 123, 125. Cf. Regin Prenter, *Spiritus Creator*, translated by John M. Jensen (Philadelphia: Muhlenberg Press, 1953), pp. 41, 69 ff., 96 f., and Gordon Rupp, *The Righteousness of God, Luther Studies* (London: Hodder and Stoughton, 1953), pp. 30-32, 182-183.

The release of the slave becomes valid by a declaration on the part of the former owner. It is therefore a purely forensic or declaratory act. The relationship between master and slave is by no means completely severed, a tie of loyalty remains. The master becomes now a protector and the freed slave has no obligation to him, yet a fundamental change in the status of the slave has occurred. . . . Before his release the slave was an object and only by manumission does he become a personality. He changes from an object of legal action to a subject capable of legal action. . . . Here also a mere declaration, a simple word, has created a new life. At least in legal theory, a new personality has been created *ex nihilo*. . . . Can we doubt that the mere word of pardon spoken "in Christ," with which the *usu forensi* calls us out of the slavery of our nomological existence, is capable of producing an ethos that really is new?[5]

CRITICISMS

Both views, which the informed reader will readily recognize as abbreviated or even caricatured for reasons of contrast, leave much to be desired. Whether it assumes its peculiar shape in Roman Catholic piety, in certain circles of Lutheranism, or in a crass sectarian perfectionism, the first view has as its consequence the identification of the rebirth with a gradually increasing goodness.[6] The result of such an identification is that the life of the believer is viewed as unambiguous. If the believer sins (as indeed he does, according to the majority holding this view), it is not because he does not always possess a good will, but simply because that good will is not always mobilized, that is, it is not always appropriately joined to its object, to the good deed.[7] Since the life of the believer is conceived as being without any radical tension which could result from his existence "in the

---

[5]Werner Elert, *The Christian Ethos*, translated by Carl J. Schindler (Philadelphia: Muhlenberg Press, 1957), p. 210.

[6]This identification of the new man with converted man is by no means limited to the theologians. While on a summer's retreat, two girls in attendance at a Bible school spied their instructor clad in swimming trunks and on his way to the water. As he approached, one was heard to say to the other: "Can't you just see he's a Christian!" Freud aside, and allowing for the impressionability of young females, the incident is at least indicative of a tendency to regard the new life of the Christian as demonstrable and measurable.

[7]Cf. S. Thomae Aquinatis, *Summa Theologiae*, Quaestio LXXV, Articulus 2, p. 348.

flesh," it follows that the imperative, the command, the summons (e.g., "put off the old man," "mortify your bodies," etc.) does not address itself to the existence of the believer as such, and for that reason does not enjoy any real relationship with the indicative (e.g., "how shall we who are dead to sin live any longer therein?" etc.), but loosed from the indicative is calculated merely to evoke the good deed, the desire for which is already present in the believer.

Whether or not the second view can properly be assigned to Melanchthon,[8] it is clear that it has its home in the so-called theory of the "legal fiction," according to which God "imputes" or credits to the sinner's account the merits won by the substitutionary "satisfaction" of Christ. The danger here, of course, is that God is cast in the role of an implacable foe who requires satisfaction at the hands of Christ before he can enter into fellowship with man. Of greater significance, however, is the fact that in its reaction to the idealism characteristic of the first view, this idea, though it asserts the divine sovereignty and transcendence in the matter of conversion,[9] by abstracting justification from human existence *(in foro coeli!)*, renders the believer's existence as new only in prolepsis, in anticipation, "in principle," and not in fact.[10] If in the first view it is the imperative which does not address itself to the existence of the believer and thus does not enjoy real relationship with the indicative, in this view it is the indicative which suffers such an inconsequence. Man remains as he was—the divine activity is reduced to a merely metaphysical basis for an ethical reformation of life.

In both views, however, the result is ultimately the same:

8Cf. the statements of Holl, *op. cit.*, pp. 118, 125-128 and Prenter, *op. cit.*, pp. 62 f. with those of Eduard Ellwein, *Vom Neuen Leben, Forschungen zur Geschichte und Lehre des Protestantismus* (Munich: Chr. Kaiser Verlag, 1932), pp. 102-109.

9Yet Holl writes that this view "would inevitably lead us to ask why God does not impute Christ's merits to all, and not merely to a few. The reply would have to be, because some believe and others do not. But that would only mean that it is faith as man's endeavor which causes God to allow Christ's righteousness to be reckoned to him. In that case it would have been earned." Holl, *op. cit.*, p. 129.

10Hence the reaction of the mystic Osiander and his modern counterpart Erich Seeberg. Cf. the latter's *Luthers Theologie in ihren Grundzügen* (Stuttgart: W. Kohlhammer Verlag, 1950), pp. 118-119.

by characterizing either the imperative or the indicative as a kind of inconsequence, the divine initiative in the *total* salvation event is lost sight of, and the believer's existence, aside from that initial act of grace in the bestowal of the *habitus* or in the "analytic" judgment, is wrested from the sphere of the divine activity and is carried on independently. And to the degree such independence is presupposed for the new life, to that degree it is catapulted into the sphere of the legal. For in that area of the believer's independence the imperative enjoys autonomy, i.e., it encounters him solely as demand. Indeed, without the "encouragement" of the command, how could he strive toward his future goal?[11] Ultimately, then, it makes no difference whether the indicative or the imperative is accorded the true grasp of reality: some aspect of the believer's existence is granted independence. But this can only result in an autonomy for the imperative which in turn issues in attributing to faith the significance of a work,[12] thus removing the new life from the sphere of grace and setting it within the framework of law and merit.

THE ESCHATOLOGICAL SETTING

Is it possible to reconcile these two interpretations of the new birth, as real change and as future goal, but without falling prey to the moralism which plagues them both? Is it possible to wed the indicative with the imperative, or must we regard them as representing a real antinomy in the New Testament; the one, perhaps, describing the new life from the viewpoint of God and the other from the viewpoint of man?[13]

When we put our question in another form: Where in the Bible does the idea of a present possession live in a harmony with the idea of a future goal, then we are immediately thrust into one specific area of biblical thought, i.e., the escha-

---

11It is precisely such reasoning which in Lutheran circles has given rise to the interpretation of the "third use" of the law as a "rule and guide for Christian conduct." Cf. e.g., *An Explanation of Luther's Small Catechism* (Philadelphia: The United Lutheran Publication House, 1935), p. 42.
12And in case of the second view, without the *habitus* of an Aquinas!
13Hans Lietzmann, *Einführung in die Textgeschichte der Paulusbriefe an die Römer, Handbuch zum Neuen Testament* (Tübingen: J. C. B. Mohr, 1928), pp.66-67.

tological. For, however the content of eschatology may be
described (and such descriptions are so numerous as to produce despair in anyone concerned with an unequivocal
definition), it is common conviction that its stock-in-trade
is precisely this relation of the "now already" to the "not
yet." For example, these two aspects are both found in
Jesus' preaching of the kingdom. On the one hand, Jesus
describes the kingdom as a present reality. His ministry
begins with the announcement that the kingdom has come
(Matt. 3:2). He declares that his exorcism of the demons
signals the penetration of God's rule within alien territory
(Matt. 12:28 ff.). His statement in Luke 10:18 ("I saw
Satan fall like lightning from heaven") has an equivalent
force. The kingdom is further described as vested in Jesus
by God and in the disciples by Jesus (Luke 22:29 f.). It is
a present good after which a man strives (Matt. 6:33; Luke
12:31), and for the sake of which he will leave his house and
family (Luke 18:29). On the other hand, Jesus announces
that the kingdom will come, i.e., that its appearance is dependent upon a future cataclysmic intervention of God in
the arena of space and time. Jesus' statements in Mark 9:1
and Matthew 16:28 have this apocalyptic feature. Both these
aspects of Jesus' preaching belong to the oldest stratum of the
Gospel tradition; neither may be dismissed as secondary.[14]
The relation between present and future, moreover, may not
be expressed in terms of "tension" or juxtaposition as in the
case of contradictories or opposites. Nor can their relation
be expressed in terms of one's deriving its significance from
the other. The present is a reality, but a reality which by
virtue of its intrinsic energy cannot be viewed as static but
rather as unfolding in its character. The kingdom has come;
it is not present merely in prolepsis or anticipation; it is
here, but because of its dynamic, it "grows." This is the
emphasis in such parables as that of the sower, the self-
growing seed, the mustard, and the leaven in Mark 4, Mat-

14Rudolf Bultmann, *Die Erforschung der synoptischen Evangelien* (6th ed.; Berlin:
Alfred Töpelmann, 1960), p. 50.

thew 13, and Luke 8. And even when the goal or consummation of the kingdom is described, as, e.g., in the Apocalypse, the writer is prevented from describing even that goal in terms of rest or cessation because of that dynamic without which the kingdom would not be reality. If the locale appropriate to the idea of the rebirth is eschatology, then the relation between the rebirth as real change and as future goal, between indicative and imperative, must be construed in terms of that same dynamic which characterizes the relation between the present and future aspects of the kingdom.

Paul's classic exposition in Romans 6 indicates first of all that the new birth is not a mere ethos issuing from a change in status. In Baptism, the believer's incorporation into the death and life of Christ is a present reality; the essential decision concerning his new existence has already been made. Paul's use of the aorist and perfect tenses, denoting completed actions, makes this amply clear: "we . . . died to sin" (v. 2); "all of us . . . were baptized into his death" (v. 3); "we were buried . . . with him" (v. 4); "we have been united with him" (v. 5); "our old self was crucified with him" (v. 6); "we have died with Christ" (v. 7); "consider yourselves dead to sin and alive to God" (v. 11);[15] "[you] have been brought from death to life" (v. 13); "you who were once slaves of sin have become obedient" (v. 17); "having been set free from sin, [you] have become slaves of righteousness" (v. 18); "you have been set free from sin and have become slaves of God" (v. 22). These expressions describe a redemption which has already occurred, not a modest beginning which a man must supplement by his own activity.

In the next breath, however, Paul points his readers to a future: "we shall certainly be united with him in a resurrection like his" (v. 5);[16] "we shall also live with him" (v. 8);

---

[15]The phrase "consider yourselves, etc." is not to be construed in the sense of a mere comparison, but as a result.

[16]The dative, which the RSV renders "in a death like his . . . in a resurrection like his," is not an instrumental but rather a societal dative, i.e., Baptism is not a copy of Christ's dying and rising, but is immediately related to his person. On the other hand, cf. Friedrich Blass, *Grammatik des neutestamentlichen Griechisch*, revised by Albert Debrunner (10th ed.; Göttingen: Vandenhoeck & Ruprecht, 1959), p. 125.

"sin will have no dominion over you" (v. 14). And more—
by his use of the imperative, Paul actually summons them
to appropriate what he had just described as already theirs:
"we too might walk in newness of life" (v. 4) ; "our old self
was crucified . . . that the sinful body might be destroyed,
and we might no longer be enslaved to sin" (v. 6) ;[17] "let not
sin therefore reign in your mortal bodies" (v. 12) ; "Do not
yield your members to sin as instruments of wickedness, but
yield yourselves to God . . . and your members to God as
instruments of righteousness" (v. 13) ; "yield your members to righteousness" (v. 19). These futures in vv. 5, 8, and
14 do not have a mere logical significance. Their intimate
connection with the imperatives of vv. 12 and 13 indicate
that they are real futures. On the other hand, neither the
future nor the imperative may be viewed as placing the
previous utterances concerning the rebirth under a condition, if such utterances are to retain their force.

Justification for regarding the relationship between the
"now already" and the "not yet," between what has already
been received in Baptism and what must follow it in
terms of a dynamic unfolding (analogous to the "growth"
of the kingdom), can be seen when we examine the content
of the indicative and the imperative. In vv. 2, 18, and 22 of
Romans 6, Paul states that in Baptism the believers have
"died" to sin, are "set free" from sin; yet in vv. 11-13 he
calls them to consider themselves "dead to sin," to refuse
sin's "reign," to refuse to "yield" their members to sin. In
vv. 17-18 and 22 he asserts that his readers have "become
obedient," "slaves of righteousness," "slaves of God," but in
vv. 13 and 19 he calls them to yield themselves and their
"members" to God, to yield their members to righteousness.
The content of the indicative is thus clearly identical with
the content of the imperative. This remarkable identity of
content is further indicated in another great baptismal passage, Colossians 2: "As therefore you received Christ Jesus

---

17These aorist subjunctives have an imperative effect because of their teleological
character. Cf. Blass, *op. cit.*, pp. 207-208.

the Lord, so live in him" (v. 6). Our conclusion can only be that if the indicative and the imperative are to retain their full strength, the new existence of the believer must be regarded as consisting in nothing other than a continual appropriation of what has already been effected in his Baptism. Bornkamm writes:

> In baptism everything is given us for this life and the next; there is nothing we would need to add. The believer's obedience can press no further forward than toward that which happened to us at the beginning. It is accomplished in a continual "creeping beneath one's baptism" (Luther). In this sense we may definitely state that *baptism is the appropriation of the new life, and the new life is the appropriation of baptism.*[18]

In other words, far from constituting a mere appeal to an appropriate act or disposition, the imperative is expressive of a being, of an existence which has come about by Baptism and which consists in a progression toward a goal (viz., sanctification and eternal life, vv. 19, 22-23). Hence, the relation between the "now already" of the indicative and the "not yet" of the imperative is not to be explained negatively, in terms of the absence of a real change in Baptism or in terms of the absence of a proper realization of what has been effected in Baptism, but positively, in terms of the unfolding of an existence begun in Baptism. And inasmuch as this dynamic has its basis in the death and resurrection of Christ and nowhere else, the imperatives are not merely summons but promise. That this is a correct interpretation of the imperatives of Romans 6 is suggested by the futures of vv. 5 and 8,[19] and particularly of v. 14:

---

[18]Günther Bornkamm, "Taufe und neues Leben," *Das Ende des Gesetzes*, Paulusstudien, *Beiträge zur evangelischen Theologie*, Band 16 (Munich: Chr. Kaiser Verlag, 1961), p. 50 (Trans. mine.—R. A. H.)

[19]When Leenhardt suggests that the futures indicate that "baptism does not effect an association with the *risen* Christ," that the "new life begins *after* baptism," and thus "presupposes a new act of God, a new dispensation," or when he states that "burial with Christ *prepares* the believer for participation in the potentiality of new life which His resurrection disclosed," he lays too great emphasis upon the chronological succession of the believer's participation in Christ's death and resurrection (an emphasis he rejects in theory) and thus overlooks the dynamic aspect of the new life. (Italics mine.) Cf. Franz J. Leenhardt, *The Epistle to the Romans*, translated by Harold Knight (London: Lutterworth Press, 1961), pp. 156, 158-159, 161-162.

"sin will have no dominion over you."[20] It is this concept of the imperative as "comforting summons" and "summoning comfort"[21] which Augustine signalized in his oft-quoted prayer: "Give what Thou commandest, and command what Thou wilt."

It is thus the dynamic or unfolding nature of this new existence in face of a goal which characterizes the man who has undergone the new birth, and not an objectively verifiable deed or virtue. To be sure, the summons, though now understood as comfort and promise, remains a summons. The activity of the believer is not a matter of indifference—his new existence must become visible and concrete. For this reason Paul can call his readers to specific ethical action in Romans 12-15, and Luther in his commentary on Romans can actually distinguish three types among the baptized:

> First, there are those who are unable to endure the cross and a mortification . . . and who are unwilling to die. They belong with the robber who was crucified on the left of Christ, for they blaspheme Christ, certainly in thought, but also by what they do. Others do endure the cross but with much feeling of suffering and resistance and groaning, but yet they overcome all this and finally die willingly. They find it hard to be despised and loathed by all. They belong with the robber at the right of the cross; indeed, Christ continues to carry them with grief and pain in his body. The third group, finally, consists of those who . . . go to this death with joy. Their prototype is Christ—Christ who died crying with a loud voice . . . like the bravest hero.[22]

Paul and Luther, however, are not speaking here of an immediately perceptible renewal, a renewal which could be asserted apart from the movement of faith. This new existence, Paul writes, "is hid with Christ in God" (Col. 3:3). In his gloss on Romans 6:7-11, Luther states that "this new life cannot be experienced but must be believed. For no one

20Otto Michel, Der Brief an die Römer, Kritisch-Exegetischer Kommentar über das Neue Testament (11th ed.; Göttingen: Vandenhoeck & Ruprecht, 1957), p. 134.
21Bornkamm, op. cit., p. 47.
22Luther: Lectures on Romans, The Library of Christian Classics, translated by Wilhelm Pauck (Philadelphia: The Westminster Press, 1961), XV, 182.

knows that he lives again or experiences that he is justified, but he believes and hopes. . . ."[23] What is perceptible in the believer may even appear to deny his new existence: "In this trial and struggle, the righteous man always resembles more a loser than a victor, for the Lord lets him be tested and assailed to his utmost limits as gold is tested in a furnace."[24] It is thus this hidden character of his new birth which marks the believer's existence.

Once again, the concept of the kingdom provides us with an appropriate analogy. In the parables of the self-growing seed, the mustard, and the leaven, the initial stage is imperceptible: "The kingdom of God is as if a man should scatter seed upon the ground, and should sleep and rise night and day, and the seed should sprout and grow, he knows not how" (Mark 4:26-27) ; "the kingdom . . . is like a grain of mustard seed, which, when sown upon the ground, is the smallest of all the seeds on earth" (Mark 4:30-31) ; "the kingdom . . . is like leaven which a woman took and hid in three measures of meal" (Matt. 13:33). Not until the appearance of the sprout and shrub and leavened loaf is there recognition that what was sown and what was hidden in the three measures of meal possessed such power of realization. Not even a process of development is reckoned with—only the surprising succession of two radically different stages.[25] Similarly, the new existence of the believer hastens imperceptibly toward its ultimate realization, and only at "harvest" will the righteous "shine like the sun in the kingdom of their Father" (Matt. 13:43). The present, then, is marked by hiddenness, by an existence so deeply hidden that it often appears under the sign of its opposite, an existence whose realization can only occasion surprise. This aspect of amazement at the finale frequently appears in Jesus' synoptic utterances. In Matthew 25:37, e.g., the righteous, in reply to the invitation of the King, ask: "Lord,

23Luther, *op. cit.*, p. 184.
24*Ibid.*, p. 189.
25Cf. Joachim Jeremias, *Die Gleichnisse Jesu* (Göttingen: Vandenhoeck & Ruprecht, 1956), p. 129.

when did we see thee hungry and feed thee, or thirsty and give thee drink?"

If at this point we were to hazard a preliminary definition of eschatology as regards its content, we would define it in terms of our characterization of the new birth, viz., a dynamic yet hidden reality, an unfolding in the face of a goal perceptible only to faith and hope. It is eschatology in this sense which provides the framework for Luther's oft-repeated and oft-misunderstood reference to the believer as being sinner and righteous at one and the same time *(simul iustus et peccator)*.[26] Although Luther's reference here has its occasion in his awareness that the believer by his new birth is not raptured from this world but continues to live in it and thus may fall prey to the "powers,"[27] it is also clear that he proceeds to an eschatological interpretation of the rebirth, since he describes the believer's sin as being removed "in hope, i.e., that it is in the process of being taken away by the gift of grace which starts this removal. . . ."[28] In the light of this and similar expressions, Luther's use of such terms as "righteous by virtue of the reckoning" and "nonimputation" is to be understood.

THE NEW BIRTH AS "EXISTENCE IN"

If the new dynamic existence is hidden; if, despite the seriousness of the imperative, there is no perceptible action or disposition which distinguishes the one who has undergone the rebirth from the one who has not, how may they be distinguished? The answer to this question is crucial, for it will determine whether or not we fall back into one of the traditional errors outlined above. To begin with, one characteristic which all interpretations of the new birth have in common, and which gives the explanation for their essen-

---

26Luther, *op. cit.*, pp. 127, 322.
27It is from out of this negative context of thought that Luther discusses the hiddenness of the new existence. In this connection cf. also Bornkamm (*op. cit.*, p. 47), who regards the imperative as appropriate to the hiddenness of the new life rather than to its dynamic.
28Luther, *op. cit.*, p. 129.

tially unbiblical stance, is that they have treated the rebirth in an exclusively individualistic fashion. That is, they have regarded the new existence as applying solely to the believer as an isolated entity. The history of exegesis reveals a continual preoccupation with the new birth of the individual, from whence flow all those conclusions regarding the *habitus*, regarding the new life as new only "in principle," but also such current interpretations as that of Karl Barth, who attributes to Baptism a purely "cognitive" significance,[29] an interpretation which may in part be described as a reaction to extravagances resulting from a certain individualism within even the Reformers' doctrine.[30]

Not once, however, does Paul ever treat the subject of the new birth from an individualistic point of view. Just as the major portion of all his thought is oriented to the concept of participation, i.e., of "being in" or "with Christ," so here the idea of rebirth is set within a societal framework. For Paul, existence is always "existence in." The idea of a theoretical man, man in a vacuum, isolated from the rest of the created order (an idea dear to medieval scholasticism and orthodoxy), never enters Paul's mind. In terms of modern phenomenology, Paul conceives of man as projected over a field of being. From this standpoint of viewing man as "being in" he contrasts, e.g., the old and new humanity, the first and second Adam in Romans 5:12-21. Because the old man is man "in Adam," i.e., because he shares solidarity with the totality of unredeemed humanity, and not because he suffers from a congenital apple poisoning,[31] he experiences sin not merely as act but also as fate, as destiny. And because the new man is man "in Christ," i.e., because he enjoys member-

---

[29] Karl Barth, *Die kirchliche Lehre von der Taufe, Theologische Studien,* Heft 14 (Zollikon-Zürich: Evangelischer Verlag, 1947), pp. 18-19, 21, 24, etc.

[30] Cf. *ibid.*, pp. 13-14.

[31] It is precisely in an understanding of man as absolute, as "private person" (Aquinas) that such a view originates. Lietzmann and Bultmann accuse Paul of such a view and hence of obscuring his argument in Romans 5, because they fail to appreciate the concept of solidarity which forms the background for the Adam-Christ antithesis. Cf. Lietzmann, *op. cit.*, pp. 61-62 and Rudolf Bultmann, *Theology of the New Testament* (London: SCM Press, 1952), I, p. 252, and "New Testament and Mythology," *Kerygma and Myth,* ed. H. W. Bartsch, translated by R. H. Fuller (London: S.P.C.K., 1954), p. 7.

ship in that corporate personality whose head is Christ, he experiences faith not merely as act but also as being. This solidarity, this "being in" is not merely a psychological but rather an ontological reality for Paul, a reality, moreover, which he obviously regards as impossible to recognize apart from the revelation. In answer to the possible objection that such a view of man implies a loss of individual identity, Dietrich Bonhoeffer, in the most significant theological treatment of this subject, writes:

> . . . the being of man should be conceived neither frozen as entity nor spirited into non-entity. In either of these cases the total existence of man would, in the end, stay unaffected. No; the man we must consider is the historical man who knows himself transplanted from the old into the new humanity and who is, by membership of the new, a person re-created by Christ. . . . The person . . . is always two in one: *individual* and *humanity*. The concept of the absolute individual is an abstraction with no corresponding reality. It is not merely in his general psychology but in his very existentiality that man is tied to society. When his existence is touched (in judgment and mercy) he knows that he is being directed towards humanity. He has himself committed the sin of the old humanity, yet he knows at the same time that humanity drew him into its sin and guilt when he was powerless to resist. He is the bearer of the new humanity in his faith, prayer and affirmation, yet knows that he is borne in all his actions by the communion, by Christ.[32]

Once again it is necessary to add that for Paul this concept of man as "being in Adam" or "being in Christ" is contingent upon the revelation, since it is only in Christ that man sees his former identity with the old man and his present identity with the new, and only in faith that he views the continuity between them in terms of his creatureliness. For example, such Christological utterances as Romans 6:9-10— "For we know that Christ being raised from the dead will

32Dietrich Bonhoeffer, *Act and Being*, translated by Bernard Noble (New York: Harper and Brothers, 1961), pp. 130-131.

never die again; death no longer has dominion over him. The death he died he died to sin, once for all, but the life he lives he lives to God"—furnish Paul with the foundation for his understanding of the believer's new existence.[33]

This aspect of Paul's theology is by no means peculiar to him. A survey of the synoptic parables reveals the same aspect dominant in them. Figures such as scattered seed, the mustard shrub and its branches, the fig tree and its leaves, the wheat and the tares, the net of fishes, etc., as well as those parables which involve communities of persons (e.g., the ten virgins, the great supper, the unmerciful servants, the talents, etc.) clearly have this concept of existence-in for their background. In the interpretation of the parable of the wheat and the tares in Matthew 13:36-43, the good seed is made to represent the community of the end-time ("the sons of the kingdom," v. 38), and in at least one instance (v. 41: "The Son of man will send his angels, and they will gather out of his kingdom all causes of sin and all evildoers") the Evangelist appears to identify even the kingdom itself with that community. Similarly, the parable of the fig tree in Luke 13:6-9 applies to the nation of Israel. Few synoptic parables, in fact, do not have this feature. A brief glance at the so-called "apostolic fathers" may also be instructive. For example, the parable of the sower as well as that of the leaven in Matthew 13 underlies the eucharistic prayer of a famous second-century church manual:

> As this piece was scattered over the hills and then was brought together and made one, so let your Church be brought together from the ends of the earth into your Kingdom.[34]

To trace the concentration of modern biblical theology upon this theme, beginning perhaps with Adolf Deissmann's and Albert Schweitzer's studies on Paulinism, as well as to indicate the intimate relation between it and the concept of

---

[33]Cf. *ibid.*, pp. 132 ff. ; 164 ; 171 ff.
[34]"The Didache," 9:4 in *Early Christian Fathers, The Library of Christian Classics,* ed. Cyril C. Richardson (Philadelphia: The Westminster Press, 1953), I, p. 175.

the kingdom, would exhaust the limits of this essay. The answer to the question concerning the difference between the one who has undergone the renewal and the one who has not has been implied throughout this discussion: only in terms of a corporate, transsubjective reality, a reality independent of the individual act but nonetheless related to it as being to mode, can there be talk of differentiation. And it is this transsubjective reality, moreover, which in the case of the new humanity provides its corresponding mode with its dynamic. "In Christ" the new man goes his way to life, whereas decay and death characterize the existence of the old humanity, of man "in Adam." "Being in Christ" is thus eschatological existence, existence in view of a goal, whereas "being in Adam" is noneschatological existence, existence deflected from its goal.

THE ASSURANCE OF THE NEW BIRTH

How can a man have any assurance that he has indeed been reborn? The answer to this question is conditional upon one's view of the rebirth. When, e.g., the new birth is construed in terms of a *habitus*, an empirical advance in piety, the assurance of having been reborn rests on the recognition of certain observable acts or psychic states. Or when the renewal is construed in merely speculative fashion, as "change in status," experience of the rebirth is a mere hypothesis. In respect to the first view, we have already indicated the hiddenness or nondemonstrability of the new birth.[35] And, in respect to the second, without cognition or the knowledge of one's rebirth, without the opportunity of confessing with Paul that "I am sure that neither death, nor life . . . nor anything else in all creation, will be able to separate us from the love of God in Christ Jesus" (Rom. 8:38-39), revelation would not impinge on man's existence and the renewal would be a mere possibility of thought.[36] On

35Pp. 86-87 *supra*.
36"If redemption is not at the same time God's work and *human experience*, then there is no certainty of salvation at all." Otto Piper, *Erlösung als Erfahrung, Sammlung gemeinverständlicher Vorträge*, No. 157 (Tübingen: J. C. B. Mohr, 1932), p. 34.

the other hand, if, as we have attempted to show, the new birth is properly understood only within a sociological frame of reference, or better, within that eschatological framework of "being in Christ," then the awareness of one's having been reborn must correspond with that framework. Then the awareness of the rebirth must be an awareness of being in Christ. This means, first of all, that knowledge of the rebirth does not originate in the individual consciousness. If such were true, faith would be the begetter and not the begotten. For over one hundred years Protestantism has suffered the ravages of this type of "experiential religion" or theology of consciousness. The Christian's psychic states, however, are acts of faith and not mere religiosity only when they are expressive of that corporate existence in Christ. It is thus in community that awareness of the renewal is born. This is the force of Paul's words in Romans 8:15b-16: "When we cry, 'Abba! Father!' it is the Spirit himself bearing witness with our spirit that we are children of God." Aside from its probable suggestion of an assembly of the baptized for corporate worship,[37] this passage indicates that the knowledge of the new existence, or, as Paul puts it here, of sonship (vv. 14, 16-17), of adoption (v. 15), of being heirs (v. 17), rests upon the community of the witness of the Holy Spirit with the believers' spirit.[38] Further, that witness of the Spirit of God is not only an inward certainty given with the external, audible cry.[39] To seek the entire explanation for such a witness in "conditions . . . associated with what is called 'religious revival,' when many of the customary restraints and inhibitions are broken up,

---

[37]Lietzmann and Michel see in the "Abba! Father!" an old Aramaic invocation preserved by the primitive community in its worship and expanded in hellenistic circles. Cf. Lietzmann, *op. cit.*, pp. 83-84 and Michel, *op. cit.*, p. 168.

[38]Note the "our spirit" of v. 16. Whether or not we follow the RSV and connect the invocation with what follows in v. 16, or together with the New English Bible conclude v. 15 with the invocation (". . . a Spirit that makes us sons, enabling us to cry 'Abba! Father!' In that cry the Spirit of God joins with our spirit, etc."), a division with which all modern editors agree, it is a community of witness which is involved —the Spirit of God and "our" spirit.

[39]This appears to be the force of the RSV translation. Cf. also C. K. Barrett, *The Epistle to the Romans*, *Harper's New Testament Commentaries* (New York: Harper and Brothers, 1957), p. 164.

and the inner life is much nearer to the surface"[40] is to revert to an identification of the Spirit with man's psychic states. If, on the other hand, we view the "witness" of the Spirit as an independent event addressing the believer from without, i.e., as the proclamation of the Word of Christ; then, in harmony with our understanding of "being in Christ" we have preserved to that community of witness its transsubjective quality; and we have retained for the witness of the Spirit its character as presupposition for the witness of our spirit, and hence for assurance.[41] Then the knowledge that one is in Christ, rather than taking its origin from any kind of reflection, is the result of a direct, unselfconscious laying hold of that Word of Christ by which he joins himself to his community as body to members. Bonhoeffer writes:

> *Fides directa* is the name which has been given by traditional Protestant dogmatics to the act of faith which, though taking place in the consciousness of the person, cannot be reflected in it. It rests on the objectivity of the event of revelation in Word and sacrament; the cleaving to Christ has no need to be conscious of itself: it is in any case wholly taken up with the performance of the *actus directus.* Man is in Christ; on that account he sees neither his sin nor his death, for there is neither sin nor death in Christ; furthermore he sees neither himself nor his own faith. He sees only Christ, as his Lord and his God. Seeing Christ in Word and sacrament means seeing, in one and the same act, the risen Crucified *in* one's neighbour and in creation.[42]

This interpretation does not deny to assurance its emotional or psychic aspects; faith must involve the total man—Luther never hesitated to say that the believer should "feel" the Spirit within, and old Protestantism spoke of faith as being also reflex and discursive[43]—but by its emphasis upon the

40C. H. Dodd, *The Epistle of Paul to the Romans* (London: Fontana Books, 1959), p. 145.
41"He is the objective word which is prior to the subjective confession. We should not forget that even in Judaism the 'Holy Spirit' is a circumlocution for what God Himself or the authoritative word of Holy Scripture says." Michel, *op. cit.,* p. 169.
42*Op. cit.,* p. 181.
43Cf. Heinrich Schmid, *The Doctrinal Theology of the Evangelical Lutheran Church,* translated by Charles A. Hay and Henry E. Jacobs (Minneapolis: Augsburg Publishing House, 1961), p. 421.

initiative of the Spirit in an objective, independent event, it guarantees to the concept of being in Christ expressed in the community of witness its priority as cause and condition of the psychic acts. For "God has *sent* the Spirit of his Son into our hearts, crying, 'Abba! Father!'" (Gal. 4:6).

Finally, because the new birth retains its essentially hidden character in this life and thus awaits its full revelation in the future, the assurance which corresponds with it shares the same quality of hoping. This is clear from the verses immediately following Paul's discussion of the community of witness: "we ourselves, who have the first fruits of the Spirit, groan inwardly as we wait for adoption as sons, the redemption of our bodies. For in this hope we were saved" (Rom. 8:23-24). In other words, by reason of the dynamic of that life into which the Spirit assures the believer that he has been drawn, he awaits that future in which assurance will be transformed into sight. "For now we see in a mirror dimly, but then face to face. Now I know in part; then I shall understand fully, even as I have been fully understood."

V

Correlation of Justification and Faith in Evangelical Dogmatics

Is justification by (through) faith alone as central an issue today as it was to the Reformers? Has the great search for the all-determining essence of Christianity, pursued with such enthusiam and erudition ever since the demise of orthodoxy, been largely without decisive results because the *sola fides* of the Reformation lost its materially regulative dogmatic function? Is the doctrine of justification by faith alone still relevant to the modern man whose existential questions are not being formulated in precisely the same terms as St. Paul's and Dr. Luther's? Would it not be a mere tour de force, out of deference to biblical authority and loyalty to confessions, to argue that especially for the modern Christian the article of justification may and ought to provide the most succinct and accurate doctrinal summary of the New Testament Gospel?

The quest for the essence of Christianity initiated by liberal theologians in antithesis to orthodox scholasticism has not been terminated by any means despite the modern ascendency of neo-orthodoxy. We do not have a uniform neo-orthodoxy within Protestantism. There are many doxies that clamor as rivals for the loyalties of our minds. There are many schools of theology within which or between which

Dr. Braaten is professor of systematic theology at Lutheran School of Theology, Maywood, Ill.

one has to move. But all of them are continuing the search bequeathed to us by liberalism, and every serious theologian, whether liberal or conservative, is inescapably caught up in a searching theological venture, whose fundamental presupposition is that "it has and it has not." Only he who has can search, but he who has everything need not search. The latter type is today all but extinct. Has the doctrine of justification by faith alone come into its own through a contemporary formulation which possesses the integrity of the old substance as well as the relevance of a modern idiom? There are many Protestant theologies that speak in exalted terms about faith and believing, but how many have really captured the paradoxical significance of the *sola?* Is it still possible to penetrate to that inner core of Christianity via the message of justification? Does the doctrine of justification understood as the proclamation of the forgiveness of sins grasp the heart of the kerygmatic witness of the New Testament? It is supposed to be conceded as self-evident that Luther did not really understand the Apostle Paul, but placed in the center of Paul's theology what really for Paul was at the periphery. The alleged reason is that Paul's polemic against the Judaizers necessarily threw his theology out of focus and resulted in a disproportionate emphasis on grace through faith apart from the works of the law. The real center of Paul's thought is the new man in Christ, or his spirit-mysticism. Luther was prepared to misconstrue Paul because of his own intense struggle under ecclesiastical legalism. We can forgive Luther, but not follow him.

Not all of the above questions will be answered in this essay concerning the *articulus stantis et cadentis ecclesiae.* But they serve to provoke us to a re-assessment of what first of all is meant by the fourth article of the Augsburg Confession. It will be obvious from a brief glance at the history of Protestant theology that not all who have adhered to the formula "justification by faith alone" have meant the same thing by it. Indeed, the most opposite meanings can be imported into that phrase. It seems ironically embarrassing that the very theological tradition which has affirmed the article by which the church stands or falls has been almost as much confused and void of inner harmony as any other tradition. Slogans and agreement upon slogans are not enough. They do not have the power to shape life and thought. They must be continually interpreted through preaching and theological labor.

There are several theological events in our time which have provided the stimulus for a renewed concern over the meaning of the Reformation doctrine of justification by faith alone. The dialectical theology gained its bearings in our time through a creative rediscovery of justification as the paradoxical essence of the Christian message. Its notion of the completely objective character of the judgment of justification as an *actus forensis* emphasized the radical discontinuities between God and man, eternity and time. Justification was extricated from that immersion in the subjective processes of inner soulish piety which the dialectical theologians felt was the most vicious form of the universal human attempt to close the gap between man and God from the side of man. Modern Protestantism, when judged by the Reformation message of justification, was a sickly relapse into medieval Romanism. It was because of his radical understanding of *sola fide* that Barth could state that all religion, even the Christian religion, must stand under the divine critical judgment. And for this reason also, Brunner's attempt to give dogmatic dignity to some "point of contact" in man could result in nothing else than a "return to the fleshpots of Egypt."

Another factor that continues to generate interest in the question of justification is the prevailing uncertainty as to what Luther actually taught in contradistinction to Melanchthon and his other followers. Karl Holl challenged the traditional interpretation of Luther and stated his new views in terms of the Ritschlian distinction between analytic and synthetic justification. Luther taught an analytic justification, which not only declares man righteous, when in fact he is totally unrighteous, but makes man righteous through actual participation in the righteousness of Christ. Melanchthon it was who gave that fatal twist to justification by defining it as an objective transcendent act *in mente Dei* (synthetic judgment) without involving an actual communication of righteousness. In Holl's opinion, the forensic idea is immoral because it is a fiction. The man is said to be righteous who is unrighteous. Not even God would treat man *as though* he were something he was not. The imputation becomes dependent upon a prior impartation. Osiander, who claimed to be faithful to the early Luther, seems to be at least in part exonerated by Holl's research.

The above events are by now well known. Of more recent significance are two works which bear upon the debate between Roman Catholic and Reformation theology. Max Lackmann has sharply questioned whether Luther's doctrine of justification may be the total and final word for the Lutheran Church on the scriptural message of justification. Is Luther's doctrine broad enough to comprehend the emphasis of James? Hence, through an exegetical study of the second chapter of James, which is as fully a part of the canonical Scriptures as any epistle of Paul, Lackmann corrects Luther by emphasizing that justification must be correlated with faith *and works*. Faith is saving, but not faith *alone;* rather faith together with its works justifies. The element of ethical obedience in justification must be given back to the church by James. Paul Althaus has answered Lackmann in such a way that, while admitting on the whole the exegetical right of his statement, its force is neutralized by an appeal to the necessity of an intracanonical critical norm by which Scripture itself must be interpreted and, if necessary, corrected. James must be corrected by Paul, for James lays the foundation for the nomistic tendencies in early Catholicism. There is no escaping some form of that hermeneutical principle which orthodoxy referred to as the analogy of Scripture, minus of course the rationalistic demand for complete harmony in all parts of Scripture. Lackmann's critique finally is referred back to the prior issues of canonicity, the norm of Scripture, and general hermeneutical questions.

The other significant work which furthers the conversation between Roman Catholic and Protestant theologians is the remarkable book by Hans Küng on Karl Barth's doctrine of justification, entitled *Rechtfertigung . . . Die Lehre Karl Barths und eine Katholische Besinnung* (1957). Hans Küng, a Roman Catholic theologian, has made an extensive comparative study of Karl Barth and the Council of Trent on justification, and concludes that they are in essential agreement. Barth, in his letter to the author printed as a preface, expresses amazement at the results of Küng's research. Yet he assures Küng that he has fully and faithfully rendered the doctrine of the *Church Dogmatics*. Of course, Barth doubts that Küng has correctly interpreted the Trindentine formulae. But if he has, then the only conclusion which remains is that Barth and Trent are in agreement. Barth expresses hope that none of the readers will propose the foolish alternative either that Barth is crypto-Catholic or that Küng is crypto-Protestant. Whatever the upshot of this discussion will be, it can only bring the doctrine of justification by faith alone into greater prominence.

Will all of these evidences of renewed interest in the "material principle" of the Reformation theology serve to return it to its original position of centrality in evangelical dogmatics? Will it again become the norm of Protestant systematic theology? Paul Tillich, for example, believes that the systematic norm of theology must provide an answer to the question implied in our present situation, which is no longer "the question of a merciful God and the forgiveness of sins," but rather "the question of a reality in which the self-estrangement of our existence is overcome, a reality of reconciliation and reunion, of creativity, meaning, and hope."[1] Therefore he lays hold of Paul's doctrine of the "new creation" or "new creature" and defines the norm of theology as the "New Being" in Jesus as the Christ. This is most adequate to the modern apologetic situation. He does not mean that mercy and forgiveness are no longer part of the Christian message. Indeed, the Pauline-Lutheran idea of justification is brought into the heart of the system and controls his thought in every direction. One might even ask with sound reason whether justification as "the Protestant principle" is not the *actual* center of Tillich's entire thought, on the one hand rending "every human claim in the face of God and every identification of God and man. On the other hand, (showing) how the decadence of human existence, guilt, and despair, is overcome by the paradoxical judgment, that the sinner is just before God."[2] It may be that Protestant Christianity will again become a dynamic prophetic movement with a word of judgment and grace to proclaim. But it seems highly problematic as long as theologians are rummaging around in eschatology, ecclesiology, and archaeology for the so-called essence of Christianity. Is not the *meaning* of justification by (through) faith alone still the all-controlling principle of Christian life and thought, without which the church really stands or falls in respect to its preaching mission?

We must distinguish between what is and what ought to be. When sermons evolve out of "interesting" topics of conversation, when preaching styles itself on the pattern of "entertaining" after-dinner speaking, when pulpits belch up moralistic fragments of wisdom for today, who can say that the meaning of *sola fides* has not become a mere memory of an archaic slogan? Maybe we have even become so magnanimous that we are ready to retract the *sola fides* for the sake of peace and unity, because every historian knows

---

1Paul Tillich, *Systematic Theology* (Chicago, Ill.: University of Chicago Press, 1951 & 1957), I, 49.
2Paul Tillich, *The Interpretation of History* (New York: Charles Scribner's Sons, 1936), p. 32.

about the divisive effects it has had within Christendom—
but always only when there has been a prophet to assert it
against a human economy of salvation. The situation ought
to be different, and the meaning of justification by faith
alone may again become the source of renewal of life and
thought as it was for Paul, Augustine, the Reformers, and
here and there but not generally within post-Reformation
Protestantism. But one thing must first happen in order to
prevent the inner self-dissolving process that took place
within the article of justification itself. The reason for the
removal of justification by faith alone from the center into
the background of theology is to be found in *the way it was
developed* from Melanchthon through the periods of orthodoxy and pietism. The problematic area in the whole doctrine
lies in the way one conceives of the interrelatedness of justification and faith. In other words, what is the nature of the
correlation between justification and faith? What the fate
of the doctrine itself in evangelical dogmatics will be, only
the future can tell. But it is the thesis of this essay that the
doctrine destroyed itself, and that the cause of its self-destruction must be clearly unmasked in order that the primary condition of its restoration may be fulfilled. The intrinsic connection of the negative cause and the positive
condition will shape up clearly as we focus upon the question
of priority vis-à-vis the concepts of justification and faith.
This is not a mere question of which comes first, the chicken
or the egg.

THE HEART OF THE PROBLEM

Albrecht Ritschl, in the dogmatic part of his monumental
trilogy entitled *The Christian Doctrine of Justification and
Reconciliation*, wrote, "The meaning of the idea of faith,
and the *relation in which it stands to justification*, have indeed been accurately determined in Evangelical theology."[3]

3Albrecht Ritschl, *The Christian Doctrine of Justification and Reconciliation*, second
edition (Edinburgh: T. & T. Clark, 1902), pp. 100-101.

(Italics mine.) Nothing could be farther from the historical truth. The relation between faith and justification has been a dark, confused, and murky area in evangelical dogmatics and has been the spawning bed of such major sixteenth century controversies as the antinomian, Osiandrian, Majoristic, synergistic, and predestinarian, together with all the later and modern equivalents. We can not go into each of these controversies, but all of them ultimately can and must be reduced to the question of the nature of the correlation between justification and faith. It is no wonder that, weary from all such controversies and harried by the *rabies theologorum*, theologians sought formulae of peace and concord, which, however, could restrain the radically questioning theological mind only for a brief time. It is an oft-repeated irony of history that a vaunted virtue may prove to be the fatal flaw in a whole movement.

The fatal flaw within Reformation theology is to be found right at the root of what for Luther's thought was the fundamental and central dogma of Christianity. The doctrine of justification for Luther described the all-summarizing Word of the Gospel. In relation to this doctrine we can not yield an inch. It is by the *sententia de justificatione* that Christianity can be distinguished from all other religions, and by which alone the true form of Christianity can be preserved against all sects, Anabaptists, Sacramentarians, and Papists. Although the description of the doctrine as the *articulus stantis et cadentis ecclesiae* is probably not to be found in Luther's writings, it does accurately state his view of the matter.[4]

If justification, for Luther, was the hub and nub of the Christian faith, it must have had for him a power of meaning corresponding to the central position he claimed for it. What then did justification mean for Luther?[5] It stood firmly and indissolubly connected with the person of the acting

[4]References in Luther may be found in Karl Barth's *Church Dogmatics* (Edinburgh: T. & T. Clark, 1956), IV, Part I, 521-522.
[5]As general sources for the following interpretation of Luther I must acknowledge my indebtedness to Nygren, Aulén, Dorner, Th. Harnack, Ritschl, Barth, Brunner, *et al.*

Christ so that he not only provides the *basis* of a future individually-appropriable subjective justification, but he is objectively the justification of the world. The world *has been* reconciled to God, whether anyone consciously acknowledges that or not. The judgment of justification is pronounced first of all fully and totally upon Christ who represents the new creation, even as the judgment of condemnation is pronounced upon Adam as the representative of the old creation. Therefore those are justified who are in Christ, and those are condemned who are in Adam. The question whether they are in Christ because they are justified, or whether they are justified because they are in Christ, would have no meaning for Luther. Christ *is* our justification. He *is* our righteousness. Justification is not a transaction going on between God in heaven and the individual on earth *on the condition* that the individual first does some necessary things as a result of which he approximates to the righteousness of Christ. Christ is not a means to justification, nor is justification a means to Christ. They are one and the same—objectively.

Perhaps the most common expression in Luther for the justifying act is the forgiveness of sins. The ground of the possibility of individual forgiveness is the objective reality of forgiveness in Christ. The actuality of forgiveness in Christ who has objectively reconciled the world to God is the presupposition for every individual apprehension of God as the forgiver of sins. Forgiveness of sins is to be preached therefore as gospel, and not as law. It is, however, inevitably law to the person who is not consciously aware that God has forgiven the sins of the world in Christ and cannot believe that this means even his own sins. He is looking around for something to insinuate into the relationship between grace and sin, and the vilest form of this interposition is that he makes a merit of his believing or a virtue of his faith. Justification as forgiveness is radically gift and not achievement. Forgiveness is an enactment performed objectively once and for all in Christ, and therefore the possibility of being subjectively forgiven always rests upon the actuality of cosmic justification in Christ. Preaching, therefore, is the announcement or proclamation of this gracious counsel of God, who offers forgiveness to enemies, sinners, and the ungodly on account of Christ.

It is important to grasp the objective validity of the forgiveness of sins offered on the part of God *prior to* the human act of faith, and therefore also repentance, in order not to fall into the later errors of both seventeenth century orthodox and eighteenth century pietistic dogmatics (see below). Justification as a divine act *propter Christum* is an actual *prius* of all inward changes for the better in man. Justification is a description of the paternal pardoning heart of God going out to meet sinners with free and undeserved grace. The Gospel is the glad tidings of the divine movement of paradoxical love expressed as forgiveness of sinners, not motivated from the outside, not caused by any human action, and certainly not characterized as an *ad hoc* contingent response of God to human repenting or believing. The inward reconciliation of the paternal heart of God with sinners occurs not because of the connection of men with Christ, but because of the connection of Christ with men. The free and full forgiveness of sins is proclaimed as an objective gift of God, on account of Christ, to sinners, not *because* they repent and believe but *in order that* they may believe and repent.

But man himself must believe. He must repent and believe in order that he may personally experience the forgiveness of sins and enjoy the benefits of fellowship with God. Luther never tired of stressing that each man must do his own confessing, believing, and repenting, even as he must do his own dying. No one can do it for him. "Wie du gläubest, so geschieht dir."[6]

But here is where a certain unclarity in Luther's own manner of expressing himself could open the very door which

---

[6]Theodosius Harnack, *Luthers Theologie* (München: Chr. Kaiser Verlag, 1927), II, 345.

Luther was trying to shut and keep shut against the specters of Pelagianism, semi-Pelagianism, synergism, humanism, and nominalistic libertarianism. Luther frequently said that faith justifies, and faith alone. "Allein der Glaube machet gerecht."[7] A tension could arise between the role of God and the role of man which then must be systematically balanced in an *ordo salutis*. Salvation might become conceived of as a synthesis of two factors, one divine and one human, with the priority always, of course, reserved for the former, but the all-decisive finality conceded to the latter. Theology, then, becomes a game for experts trained in juggling the contributions of God (grace) and the contributions of man (free will) in the totality of salvation. Luther most emphatically never understood salvation in this manner, although some of his successors, especially those who never read *The Bondage of the Will*, found it possible to misconstrue his meaning. On the one hand, Luther could say that faith is a work which must be done by man, and on the other, that faith is not a work of man at all, but is a gift of the Holy Spirit. Both statements are true when seen from the right perspective. In any case, faith is a work. It is act. But how is it related to justification—as a means to an end or as the effect of a cause? In other words, how is faith correlated to justification in Luther's mind? If faith is described as a work which justifies, it could be understood to mean that God forgives my sin because I do something, because I believe or feel miserable from sin and guilt. The remission of sins is something I can get if only I fulfill certain requirements. I have only to be told what they are, and under personal persuasion I may even choose or decide to do that. This, Luther perceived, is the essential element in all false religion: "If I do thus, God will be merciful to me."[8] Strictly speaking, it would even be misleading to say that if I believe in Christ, God will be gracious to me, as if my believing is not already

---

7*Ibid.*, p. 342.
8Anders Nygren, *Agape and Eros* (Philadelphia, Pa.: Westminster Press, 1953), p. 688.

evidence of God's grace, as if my faith is not itself *created by* the forgiving grace of God while I am still a sinner. The *quid pro quo* type of connection between faith and justification was certainly not what Luther meant to affirm by his assertion that faith makes righteous, or faith justifies. But neither did Luther make it unmistakably clear that he did *not* mean that, unless one interprets his doctrines of predestination and the bondage of the will as the attempt to root out every possible misunderstanding about the nature of the correlation between justification and faith. Justification is objectively prior to faith. Faith is subjectively the result of the creative impact upon the sinner of God's acceptance of him. Therefore it may be said that faith justifies in the sense that it is the becoming aware of that forgiving love by which it was first created. Justification precedes faith, while faith is the responding acknowledgment of itself as gift and of God as gracious giver of that gift through creative forgiving love. Faith is by all means not a cause of forgiveness and not a prior condition of justification which can possibly be fulfilled by a will in bondage. It would only be possible to say that Luther reversed the relation between justification and faith, making justification dependent upon a contingent human act, if one regarded the repudiation of free will *in spiritualibus* as a heterogeneous element in Luther's mind. No one will rest a case on that possibility if he recalls that Luther frequently expressed the desire in his later life to swallow, like another Saturn, all his children, listing his book *De servo arbitrio* among the very few exceptions.

John Calvin was one of Luther's disciples who clearly saw that the Reformation could be betrayed by a secret agent working from within the article of justification to hand it back to the enemy. The publican may be the greatest pharisee of them all by exchanging the humility of his faith for the justifying grace of God. The righteousness of faith is not an alternative to the righteousness of works or of the law on the same human plane. The righteousness of faith is not a human possibility, whereas the righteousness of works is relatively attainable. Justification is not procured by faith as a human attitude or virtue (inner works) in lieu of justification by external works of piety. Faith-righteousness is as different from works-righteousness as God is from man. Faith does not prepare, anticipate, or cooperate with the divine forgiving attitude expressed in the justifying act. There is nothing at all that faith contributes in the way of completing a subjective process which culminates finally in justification. "La foi ne justifie pas entant que c'est une oeuvre que nous faisons."[9] Calvin says that it is one of the greatest blasphemies that Satan can vomit forth to claim that faith is an intrinsic virtue, power, or achievement of man which merits or earns the conciliating grace of God. The relation between grace and faith is the other way around. Grace creates faith. It creates the means by which it shall be received. Man has no power or inclination to receive. Man needs to become a new creature because he has no remaining capacity to trigger off the event which effectuates his justification.

In Luther and Calvin, then, the truth or the reality of justification as expressive of God's most basic attitude towards mankind on account of Christ is both the presupposition of the human response of faith and creative of that by which forgiveness is received. Synergism is radically excluded *in loco justificationis*. The correlation between justification and faith is strictly understood as one wherein the priority of justification is affirmed to rule out even the possibility of a fiduciary synergism.

It was an ominous turn of events when Melanchthon, in the interest of refuting the Stoic idea of necessity and of upholding the freedom of man (humanistically conceived) and ethical responsibility, inserted into the revised *Loci* of 1535 and still more clearly in the third edition of 1543 the idea that conversion results from the combination of three

---

9Karl Barth, *Church Dogmatics* (Edinburgh: T. & T. Clark, 1956), IV, Part 1, 617.

factors, the Word of God, the Holy Spirit, and the faculty of the will. Man possesses before justification the *facultas applicandi se ad gratiam*. In other places Melanchthon says that at least the human will must not resist. This is a perceptible shift from Luther's idea that the will has inherently only the ability to resist, and is in fact converted while it is resisting.

Notwithstanding all his emphasis on the forensically imputative character of justification, we already see in Melanchthon the tendency to remove the article of Justification to a position of secondary rank among all the doctrinal loci. There is a development within Melanchthon away from the "already" to the "not yet" of justification as he becomes preoccupied with the question at what point in the process of psychologico-religious experience God declares the individual to be righteous. More attention is paid to the subjective conditions that must be fulfilled before the sinner becomes justified. Justification stands at the end of a conversion process which issues in repentance and faith. Faith becomes the condition of justification. Forgiveness is what man receives after he is converted, and therefore it loses its creative character. The damage that results from making faith prior to justification forms the dark side of the history of the fate of the material principle of the Reformation through the periods of orthodoxy and pietism.

THE MATERIAL PRINCIPLE BECOMES IMMATERIAL

What brought about the steady deterioration of the doctrine of justification in the orthodox systems of theology from the *Formula of Concord* (1580) to the period of Enlightenment, in which it was all but completely obscured? It was not destined to appear again in any fashion resembling the form and function it possessed in the thought of the Reformers until its dramatic comeback in the theology of Martin Kähler. And from him it has passed into our time with decisive impact through Tillich and the dialectical theologians. What happened to it in the meantime?

Luther had regarded the article of justification as not merely a single article among many others, but as the foundational truth with generative power for the entire organism of Christian faith, life, and thought. The relative importance of any Christian doctrine was determined by its proximity to this central article of faith. All doctrines, in fact, must somehow be corollaries of the vital principle of justification. But it gradually came to assume an increasingly inferior position in the theology of the orthodox fathers of the seventeenth century. While it would be an exaggeration to say that it suffered the death of complete irrelevance, it is certainly true that it was threatened by a serious abridgment of its rights.

The first step in the process of relegating the material principle to a subordinate place (locus) was the rending asunder of what had been indissolubly united in the Reformation, namely faith and the Word of God, or in other words, the formal (*sola scriptura*) and the material (*sola fide*) principles. The effect of this finally took the shape of the orthodox defense of a *theologia irregenitorum* against the insistence of the pietists on personal participation in the object of one's theologizing. The assurance of being justified through faith became transmuted into a dogma (and one among many others) whose validity was to be derived by prior demonstrations of the sole authority of Scripture. Justification by faith is a true doctrine because it is taught in the Scriptures. (Shouldn't one rather say that it is taught in the Scriptures because it is true?) Hence the faith principle is no longer of co-ordinate rank with the Scripture principle, as was the case in the Reformation. The two principles which had enjoyed relations of mutual dependence in the Reformation synthesis now drew away from each other because of the peculiar *polemical* requirements of the age. On the one side was Roman theology, which rejected the faith principle as arbitrary private fancy, yet seemingly shared a common basis for polemics with the Protestants in their acknowledgment of the divine authority of the Holy Scriptures. On the other side were the fanatical enthusiasts who spiritualized, and therefore nullified, the authority of Scripture by taking complete recourse to inward gnosis and feeling. This also seemed to bear out the Roman charge that mere faith leads to private fancy. Therefore, pressures converging from opposite sides provided the occasion for disrupting the harmonious co-ordinate relation between the formal and material principles, with an obvious detrimental effect upon the latter.

Justification as a doctrine essentially descriptive of the reassuring ground of personal salvation, so important to the Reformers, gradually underwent a transformation until it became one of many true doctrines in the orthodox system *(fides quae creditur)*, which, moreover, one could know *(notitia)* and assent to *(assensus)* without the personal experience of salvation *(fides specialis* or *fiducia)*. The assurance grounded in the reality of justification itself became instead a logical dogmatic inference from the possession of pure doctrine *(reine Lehre)*, which could be established pior to the event of personal involvement in salvation. Hence the possibility and even the necessity of a *theologia irregenitorum*, the very whispering of which fell like blasphemous thunder upon the ears of many pious people. In this way the material principle of the Reformation was deprived of significant rank within the citadel of faith, and the way was prepared to give it one of many places beside others.

Committing an error imperceptible to itself, seventeenth century so-called orthodox theology had landed in a full-fledged intellectual form of Pelagianism. The works of the intelligent were substituted for the good works of the medieval church inasmuch as the theology of the unregenerate has the same objective content as the theology of the church. And this can and must be known and assented to as free human acts before the experience of being justified unto a new life in Christ. The sequence *notitia—assensus—fiducia*, as it was developed, is pure Pelagianizing intellectualism. It is a naïve and shallow view of history to credit or blame (depending on one's point of view) the collapse of orthodoxy upon external attacks. Rather, Protestant orthodoxy was internally undermined because it betrayed the very principle by which it was originated and upon which it ought to have built.

POST-REFORMATION THEOLOGY

The plain result of depriving justification of its methodological function in laying the foundation for the whole of systematic theology was the fact that now justification had to be given a special place somewhere in the superstructure as one in a series of loci. However, the fate of irrelevance which justification suffered is not fully explicable by the fact that dogmatics in general had not yet advanced scientifically beyond the "local" method. Even this method could have given justification the first place instead of putting it somewhere towards the end of the whole process of salvation.

With but few exceptions, the seventeenth century divines strictly defined justification as an *actus Dei forensis in foro coeli*. It effects no change *in* man; it is external, forensic, and imputative. Today we might regard the juridical categories as too limiting of the full meaning of justification, for while a judge's objective declaration may release the accused from the negative consequences of crime before the law, this act does not by itself establish personal fellowship of the most intimate kind between the judge himself and the accused. Yet the intent or content of the doctrine is positively essential to the Christian faith. It makes grace wholly independent of merit and undergirds faith in the sovereign freedom, power, and love of God. But precisely herein lies the glaring contradiction in the whole orthodox *ordo salutis*. The inner meaning of justification, even as held by the orthodox, should have guaranteed the doctrine a place at the head of the whole process of salvation, as the transcendent foundation within the love of God, who for the sake of Christ forgives the sinner and justifies the ungodly, independent of and prior to any change in man. That loving, forgiving concern of God should be seen as the cause of the inner changes in man. But now, by being located at the end of a series, justification surprisingly is made to depend upon a change in man. How so? Simply by making faith a productive condition of justification.

The question is asked: If faith is the prior condition of justification, how does a man come to faith? The *ordo salutis* sets this forth. The first error occurs at the moment a distinction is made between prevenient grace and justifying grace, according to which the former first liberates the will, and then, in virtue of the mutual cooperation of both, God responds with the remission of sins. Rather, prevenient grace is from the first based upon justification. Therefore justification should stand at the very head of the *ordo salutis*, instead of being postponed to an inferior place. Hadn't Luther conceived of justification as the crucial point of transition from the old to the new life? The orthodox systems, on the other hand, made justification depend upon the new life. *Vocatio, illuminatio, regeneratio,* and *conversio,* including repentance and faith, are placed prior to justification. Thus we have the anomaly that regenerated and converted persons are not yet justified! Justification is a mere effect contingent upon the previous factors.

The contradiction is apparent. Justification is rigorously defined as an *actus Dei forensis* nondependent upon a moral change for the better in man, in order to exclude anxious questionings of a troubled conscience over the righteousness of works, yet in the system its belated position makes it wait upon a whole series of inner acts and changes wrought *in* man. What was gained is thereby lost. If repentance and faith are necessary subjective conditions preceding justification, then what of the troubled soul who asks whether his repentance is deep enough and his faith true enough to result in acceptance at the divine tribunal?

There would be a way out of this dilemma if a distinction had been made between the objective reality of justification and the subsequent subjective faith-consciousness of that reality. But since no such distinction was made, faith became a condition of justification rather than justification the creative ground of faith.

THE CRITERION IN BAPTISM

Gustav Aulén has called Baptism the Sacrament of prevenient love.[10] This was also the prevailing conviction in orthodox dogmatics. But here was a special problem. How could the *ordo salutis* be developed so as to maintain coherent relation between infant Baptism and adult conversion, i.e., so as to avoid the appearance of a double way of salvation? They were uneasy about taking refuge in Luther's artificial assertion of an infantile faith. It is rather farfetched to say that week-old babies believe in Jesus Christ. The orthodox solution was as follows. Regeneration takes place in Baptism, not on the prior condition of infantile faith but in order that faith may be produced. This statement of the matter has the advantage of remaining proportionately equivalent to what happens in adult conversion. The powers of regenerating grace evoke repentance and faith in the adult. Justification then ensues upon the satisfactory fulfillment of the prior conditions, viz., repentance and faith. By making regeneration precede justification, a single *ordo salutis* could logically encompass both infant Baptism and adult conversion. But the price for such an achievement of systematic coherence was the postponement of justification until the later stages of the process of salvation.

But even at that price systematic coherence was not

10Gustav Aulén, *The Faith of the Christian Church* (Philadelphia, Pa.: Muhlenberg Press, 1948), p. 379.

achieved. For in the Lutheran doctrine of Baptism, infants are not only regenerated. They are simultaneously declared to be justified, and this, not *because* they believe, but *in order that* they may believe. In Baptism the justifying act is not delayed until the child does believe. The pardon of God rests upon this child as the creative basis of his emerging faith. Why, then, postpone justification until the adult believes? Indeed, only since God declares himself favorably disposed in forgiveness towards me is it possible for me to believe. Otherwise the motivation for God's gracious forgiveness would be found within me. Systematic coherence and the avoidance of a double way of salvation can be achieved only when justification is consistently given the place of priority. In fact, Baptism is the stone of offense to all ideas of salvation which make faith the condition of justification. Theologians end by watering it down, or they implicitly teach a double way of salvation on the grounds that with God all things are possible. Baptism, in Lutheran theology, provides *the* criterion of a correct doctrine of justification—or at least it acts as a sure symptom.

LATENT THOMISM

A suspicious approximation to the Roman medieval conception of salvation had taken place unwittingly. We can only suggest what would require a lengthy dissertation to prove. In order to avoid complex subtleties we shall bypass the difficult question of variations between the Scotistic and Thomistic teachings. Our purpose will be served just as well by taking as the standard of comparison St. Thomas' doctrine of justification which is set forth in the *Summa Theologica* at the close of the *prima secundae*.

Protestants have been in the habit of characterizing the medieval idea of justification as Pelagian; but this is true only of one school of thought, namely, the nominalistic. St. Thomas' doctrine is actually far less Pelagian than is almost the whole of modern Protestantism, including many Lutheran systems, especially those standing in the pietist or humanist traditions. It is also significant that the scholastics against whom Luther revolted were nominalists and not real disciples of St. Thomas, notwithstanding the stature of a Thomist like Cajetan. It is very probable that Luther's knowledge of Thomas was very imperfect and that he did not have him specifically in mind when he branded the scholastic theologians as Pelagian. It is quite understandable therefore that when the orthodox Lutheran theologians fit their doctrine of justification into the system, they were not aware that in principle they were framing a doctrine which at the essential point was similar to Thomas' idea.

The essential point of similarity is this: forgiveness of sins *(remissio peccatorum)* does not stand at the beginning but at the end of a subjective preparatory process. The change wrought in man by this process becomes the necessary condition of justification. Man must become something other than he was before God forgives him. The inner subjective change becomes the cause, and justification becomes the effect, rather than vice versa. Even when the subjective condition is defined as repentance and faith, the matter becomes no better, for then the *sola gratia* becomes fractured to the extent that it is man who repents and believes.

The parallel between the orthodox Lutheran and the Thomist doctrines extends still further. Both conceive of a *gratia praeveniens* which produces the inner change that is necessary before the sinner may be declared righteous in the sight of God on account of Christ's merits. But in doing this both made a damaging distinction between prevenient grace and justifying grace. Is prevenient grace some kind of magical "mana" power? Is it not precisely identical with justifying grace? Is not justifying grace the creative power of a paradoxical love which goes to meet the sinner where he is, without waiting for the sinner to be elevated to a higher level through prior manifestations of repentance and faith? But both the orthodox Lutheran and the Thomist doctrines presuppose that an inner change must first be wrought in man before God will justify him. Therefore justification in both systems is accorded secondary status in the sequence of dogmatic thought. Both of them too, with some right, could claim to be escaping the charge of Pelagianism because they laid great stress on the initiating grace of God without which man can do nothing. But the point is simply this: the initiating or prevenient grace (Thomas says *infusio gratiae*) is given in order to make possible some development within man which by the cooperation of his will finally elicits the forgiving favor of God. There can be no doubt about the truth of this judgment inasmuch as *notitia* and *assensus* are made essential elements in *fides justificans*, though both involve a positive response of the will *before* the same will has experienced the effects of regeneration or justification. (What kind of will is it which is neither "bound" nor regenerated? What would Luther have said?)

Protestants have tended to overlook this most significant point of similarity between their own doctrine and the Thomist version because they have been too busy finding fault with the medieval *idea* of grace. They have charged it with being impersonal and magical, substantialistic and quantumistic, and everything else that is supposed to be so bad. But they have missed the point altogether and have thought that by psychologizing and personalizing grace they have found completely adequate symbols by which to conceptualize God's relation to man. This is not the real issue between evangelical dogmatics and Roman theology, however careful we must be in guarding against subpersonal categories in conceiving of God's relation to man. (We must be equally careful not to limit God to personal categories. Even in evangelical circles a *kataphatic* theology must be yielded its rights for the sake of the sovereignty of God.) The real issue consists in the meaning, place, and function of the doctrine of justification by grace alone through faith alone, namely, the question of priority in the correlation of justification and faith. Seventeenth century Lutheran theology, from this perspective, absorbed into itself a latent Thomism, and ever since evangelical theology has had to labor as a victim of this error.

ELECTION AND FAITH

The most painful effect of the false understanding of the nature of the correlation between justification and faith is evident in the election controversies that have harassed the Lutheran Church. Article XI of the *Formula of Concord,* concerning God's eternal foreknowledge and election, was written, as is stated in the introductory paragraph, not to settle an existing dispute among the theologians of the Augsburg Confession, but "by the aid of divine grace to prevent disagreement and separation on its account in the future among our successors." Why did it fail to serve its self-avowed purpose? I believe the chief reason is that in the pursuant dogmatics, from J. Gerhard to D. Hollaz, the article of justification no longer provided any basis for the assurance as long as the notion prevailed that faith is the condition of justification and justification is the effect of faith. Therefore, those fearing a conditioned salvation sought to compensate for the downgrading of justification by investing all their interest in the doctrine of election. Since assurance could no longer be gained by correlating faith and justification, it was sought by correlating election and faith. This is further proof that the article of justification lost its position of centrality.

However, the seventeenth century theologians failed to gain any assurance even from the doctrine of election because they interpreted election (predestination) as an act of God dependent upon his foreknowledge. Almost all of the orthodox Lutheran divines (Gerhard, Quenstedt, Calov, Hollaz, Baier, *et al.*) reduced election to God's foresight of those who would persevere in faith to the end (*intuitu fidei finalis*). He elects those whom he foresees will come to and remain in faith. Faith is the condition of both election and justification. This is in direct opposition to the *Formula of Concord* (Article XI) which clearly teaches that God not only foresees, but he "sees to it"; he not only predestines the *conditions* of salvation, but he predestines *sinners* unto salvation.

The doctrine of election *ex praevisa fide* or *intuitu fidei finalis* has been the main form of teaching held by Lutheran theologians since the *Formula of Concord* and has been accepted as the second possible form of teaching alongside of Article XI of the *Formula* (Form I) by the American Norwegian synods that merged in 1917. The practical issue at stake in these two forms of doctrine is simply whether a contemporary Lutheran Church will allow sufficient latitude so as to maintain continuity with the seventeenth century theologians as well as the sixteenth century confessional statements. What is most unreasonable and inconsistent is the position taken by some modern Lutheran opponents of the "second form" who make its rejection a criterion of altar and pulpit fellowship while pledging unbroken doctrinal allegiance to the seventeenth century theology which authored that teaching. They have "fellowship" with the past adherents of the "second form" but not with the living ones.

But aside from the practical implications of the two forms for the church, there is the question of theological truth, which may not be sacrificed for church-political expediencies. Many have taken, and will take, a "don't rock the boat" attitude. Theological issues become things with bargaining power under the control of negotiating committees. But theology can not abdicate its right to raise again the systematic question of ultimate truth.

It seems to me that adherents of both forms of teaching create an insoluble problem for themselves by making justification an effect of faith. If justification is an effect of faith, then faith is a cause of justification; and if this is true, however strongly we urge that it is not a meritorious cause but only an instrumental cause, then the whole burden of salvation finally rests upon relative and temporal conditions in history and human existence. The final link in the chain of salvation is forged by a human decision and historical contingency. Saving the situation (i.e., avoiding semi-Pelagianism) by adding, in qualification, that faith is a gift of God is based on a true insight if seriously meant; but then it must lead us to wonder why justification is not understood as the creative cause of faith, prior to it, rather than the mere effect of it and subsequent to it.

The recent Lutherans (so-called "Missourians" *et al.*) who have seen synergism in the *intuitu fidei* form of doctrine would agree with Schaff who speaks of a "refined evangelical modification of semi-Pelagianism." They have seen that this doctrine finally places the burden of salvation upon the good will of man and therefore leaves it suspended in mid-air. There is no assurance of salvation. But in their struggle for assurance they have unfortunately shifted the emphasis in Lutheran theology from justification to election. This they had to do because they simply inherited a tradition which had already deprived justification of any real significance.

If election is understood as the dimension of depth in our justification, then we will not make election one thing and justification another. There is continuity between them; both of them constitute the basis of faith. If election is understood as the eternal ground of our justification in Christ, the actuality (not the mere possibility) of which is received through faith, then we will not do as the Calvinists and some Lutherans do, namely, develop an aprioristic metaphysic of the eternal decrees of the will of God. It will be left as Article XI of the *Formula* leaves it, a corollary of our assurance that God justifies us as sinners. It is a statement of faith *(Glaubensgedanke)* and for faith. Election is not a speculative doctrine embedded in a deterministic metaphysics; it is a datum of the Christian consciousness rooted in the existential awareness of the strictly derivative character of faith. We could call the doctrine of election a phenomenological description of faith's certainty that it owes all that it has and *is* to God, without making God the father and free will the mother of faith itself. That is why Luther said to Erasmus that it is more Christian not even to use the term "free will" because ultimately it is blasphemy and the essence of irreligion.

It is common knowledge that the doctrine of election *ex praevisa fide* was developed as an alternative to the Calvinist absolute double predestinarianism. It was an attempt to explain quite rationally the mystery of election by making it dependent upon whether or not man accepts or rejects. But if theology is not going to abandon its existential ground, then it has no business addressing itself to a non-existential question, as was done: why are some elected in preference to others *(cur alii prae aliis)*? The rational answer is that some are elected because it was foreseen that they would believe; others were not elected because it was foreseen that they would not believe. Election in this reasoning is void of content. There are two other possible answers equally as neat. One is the double predestinarian, which simply says that for no reason whatsoever God elected some to be saved and others to be damned. The other is the universalist (ἀποκατάστασις) teaching, based on some Pauline passages, which says that all are elected unto salvation. All of them say more than the doctrine of election is prepared to say. Article XI of the *Formula* does not speculate about those outside of the circle of faith. And for a very good reason. Election can only affirm faith's certainty that it is derived totally from the will and acts of God, that being forgiven while we were yet sinners is the creative reason of faith. It says nothing about those allegedly outside of faith. It says nothing about a horrible decree or about the equally "horrible" decision required of man *in order to* be saved. It is therefore the death of every *Entscheidungstheologie*. From this perspective, election is another way of talking about justification pressed to its ultimate eternal ground. Election is eternal justification.

Many are afraid of this type of doctrine because it supposedly makes faith a passive thing and leads to quietism. It does nothing of the sort. It is precisely those who hold to the *intuitu fidei* or *ex praevisa fide* doctrine who emphasize what a passive thing faith is in order thereby to avoid the stigma of synergism. Faith is an active thing. Grace personalizes man; it does not encounter him already as a person. Grace finds man irresponsible and makes him responsible. Grace finds man in bondage and makes him free. Grace is creative; it is not merely persuasive. The unbelieving sinner is not inert like a log or a stone when forgiveness is proclaimed to him. He is active, but negatively so. By nature he can only resist the Spirit of God, and when he is declared forgiven because of Christ he becomes converted, if at all, against and in spite of his perverse will (Luther). Karl Barth states it perfectly when he says, "Man acts when he believes, but that he believes when he acts, this is God's act."[11] Faith is an "impossible possibility." Or Gogarten states it equally well when he says that faith is not a function of "this side" which takes to itself "the other side"; "it is itself something from the other side; it is a miracle." Faith itself "belongs to revelation."[12] It is not a human possibility predicated upon some remnant of the *imago Dei* in man. The point of contact *(Anknüpfungspunkt)* in man is not will, reason, or feeling. We have only to affirm the correlation between grace and sin, reconciliation and estrangement. Only in this way can we prevent the *sola fides* from falling into contradiction with the *sola gratia*. Both can be affirmed meaningfully only by maintaining the priority of justification in its correlation with faith. And election will lose its frightening aspects when it is understood as the dimension of depth in our justification. The Calvinist and Arminian

---

11Karl Barth, *Die Lehre vom Worte Gottes* (München: Chr. Kaiser Verlag, 1928), p. 258. Quoted by Paul Lehmann. *Forgiveness* (New York: Harper and Brothers, 1940), p. 160.
12Friedrich Gogarten, *Von Glauben und Offenbarung* (1923), pp. 48-52.

errors, as well as their Lutheran analogues, will be avoided, and a way which transcends the alternative between the usual two forms of the doctrine of election can be developed without nullifying the genuine concerns in each of them.

THE PRESENT SITUATION

We began our essay by indicating the reasons for a renewed interest in the doctrine of justification. There are real grounds for hope that not only theology, but the living church itself, will again find it necessary to stand upon the meaning and substance of this doctrine, when all its other stances prove themselves impotent. Of course, if this happens, theology itself can not claim all the credit, but it will have the humility to see the Spirit of God working through contemporary events and movements to force the church to live again from the divine fiat.

Catastrophic world-historical events and existentialism in philosophy, literature, and art, together with modern depth psychology, have made their contributions toward the possibility of a new vital restatement of the doctrine of justification rooted in the experience of divine forgiveness. Modern empirical studies of man by the methods of psychoanalysis, phenomenology, and existentialism have placed in the shadows the older shallow humanism that theologians courted in developing a theological anthropology. They also provide new categories, concepts, and a relevant vocabulary which may aid theologians in their constructive work.

A good example of how fruitful the results can be when theology remains open to these newer studies is Paul Tillich's reformulation of the doctrine of justification by grace alone through faith alone. Phrases like "forgiveness of sins" and "justification through faith" can be enriched by the idea of "acceptance" that is adopted in the psychotherapeutic situation. The Lutheran formula that "he who is unjust is just" in the eyes of forgiving love may be given the modern phrasing that "he who is unacceptable is accepted." The basis of the courage to accept oneself as one happens to be is the assurance that one has been accepted in spite of one's unacceptableness. Faith is simply the acceptance of one's acceptance. "There is nothing in man which enables God to accept him."[13]

This new formulation of the old doctrine has a bearing on our argument for the priority of justification over faith. In the psychoanalytic situation the healer does not say to the patient, "I'll accept you as you are if only you'll accept me first." That illustrates what folly it is to make justification dependent upon faith. The healer simply accepts the patient though he is unacceptable. And only because he is first accepted is it possible for the patient to accept himself even though he feels himself unacceptable. The fact that God accepts us as we are, namely, as sinners, is the creative ground of our accepting acceptance, of receiving the forgiveness of sins. Justification as an objective event must precede the subjective side of receiving by faith what God offers. Justification is prior to faith.

13Paul Tillich, *Systematic Theology* (Chicago, Ill.: University of Chicago Press, 1951 & 1957), II, 179.

VI

Concept of Selfhood in the New Testament and Modern Ethics

DAVID M. GRANSKOU

The problem of this paper is called forth by some of the modern discussions on selfhood. There is a need to evaluate the modern quest for selfhood in the light of the Christian faith. The difficulty is to determine the right course for this discussion. One contemporary Christian attempt to solve the problem has dovetailed Christianity and modern psychology as much as possible. This approach holds that it is the mature Christian who comes to a full sense of selfhood. Another segment of modern Christianity is preaching the ethic of selflessness or self-denial. The debate has therefore ranged from the position of uniting religion with psychology to that of setting religion against psychology.

The need of today is for a frank discussion of the Bible and psychology. There is, of course, no biblical psychology as such. The needed investigation is rather into the psychological implications of the biblical frame of reference implied in the Bible, that is, an ontology based on the creative purpose of the living God in covenant with his people.

This type of study is needed, for it will meet head-on what much of the present interest in the union of religion and psychology side-steps, namely, the starting point of

DR. GRANSKOU is secretary of the Department of Theological Cooperation, National Lutheran Council, New York City.

125

biblical religion. While modern research in psychology has started from the self-consciousness of man, the biblical point of view starts with God and his search for man.

Selfhood has many aspects. In a fuller discussion of the problem all these aspects could be pursued. This article will aim at opening up two aspects of the problem: first, the religious aspect of selfhood; and secondly, the social aspect. The religious aspect of selfhood is the relation of the self to God, and the social aspect is the relation of the self to the religious group.

Let us provisionally define selfhood as the consciousness of one's personality as distinct from others, and as the reality of this awareness in the individual's being able to assert his distinction. This is different from such terms as egocentricity, or selfishness, which could imply a concern for the self that might not involve self-awareness or self-assertion. These two factors of awareness and assertion of the ego make up the selfhood.

The problem is: Can Christianity and the belief in Jesus Christ and membership in his church promote or hinder the development of selfhood? This is not an easy question, and it has been answered both ways. Both Christian and non-Christian thinkers have held that Christianity and selfhood do not mix. Generally the non-Christian reasoning suggests that the relation of man to God is through some type of mystical union or stoic subordination to the will of God. From this standpoint the charge is that mysticism lessens self-awareness, and that a stoic subordination to God lessens self-assertion.

Two men who have made such contentions are Nietzsche and William James. Both have a following in modern thought. Nietzsche's attack on Christianity is well known. Especially devastating is the criticism contained in his *Genealogy of Morals:* Belief in God and a system of moral laws are instruments of enslavement used against the very souls of men to make them beasts. Here in stark form is the romantic quest for life. It cannot be totally brushed aside with the *argumentum ad hominem* that Nietzsche became insane. Sigmund Freud, who was far from demented, seems to have seen a certain truth in Nietzsche. He called the belief in God a father-fixation that is restrictive to human growth. The problem arises in that Christianity stresses a form of relation and uses terminology that would qualify it as a target for Freud's charge. God is called "Father," we are to become as "little children," etc. While these facts are true, it is also true that Christianity makes claims for some sensitivity to the growth of the psychic life; for it stresses "freedom," "forgiveness of sins," and the like. Thus there is room for a clash of opinion.

From another angle, William James has grouped all religions of a personal type into a form of mysticism. For James the ecstasy of mysticism is not in line with the development of healthy men who can face the problems of life. For him the experince of the mystics involves the loss of selfhood. He quotes Plotinus as typical: "He changes, he ceases to be himself . . . absorbed in God, he makes but one with him." And yet the empiricism of James shows up some interesting contradictions. After stating that personal religion, including Christianity, is not for the healthy soul he observes: "Strange that a species of book so abundant among ourselves should be so little represented elsewhere—the absence of strictly personal confessions is the chief difficulty to the purely literary student who would like to become acquainted with the inwardness of religions other than Christian."[1]

Thus from James' point of view there are two contrary elements that are observed in the Christian faith. Theoretically he sees all God-man relations in personal religion as mysticism and tending to the loss of selfhood. Practically he cannot deny the empirical fact that Christianity is unique for its literature of introspection. This

---

[1] W. James, *The Varieties of Religious Experience* (New York: Random House, 1902), p. 393.

observation is in line with the modern studies in the history of ideas which show that the development of personality as a philosophical concept was the work of Christianity.

How are we to consider the charges of these men, and how are we to consider the resources of Christianity at this point? Ought the Christian to deny his selfhood, or is there something out of perspective in the analysis of men like James and Nietzsche?

CHRISTIAN MORALISM

One solution to this problem, as attempted by James and others, is what he calls the "religion of the healthy-minded." This sees the positive aspect of Christianity in the moral and religious values of the faith, not in the personal God-man relationship. Thus the personal elements of Christianity would come out of the ethical and social proclamation of Jesus. It is the life of Jesus, not the worship of Jesus, that counts. The way to the development of the self is growth, freed from the morbid inhibitions of the monastery. This is in some respects attractive. In opposition to mysticism, it allows for the assertion of the individual in a religious dimension. Man is not asked to merge himself with God, but is cast on his own and has a sense of responsibility. This is health, so reasons the pragmatist.

Yet it remains to be seen if James is right in classing all personal religious relations with God as mystical. If his classification of religious experience is too restrictive, then his psychological conclusions should be re-examined. Perhaps then we can take seriously his observation that Christianity furnishes more spiritual autobiography than other religions. This may mean that Christianity is not so much a self-annihilating mysticism as James thought. Another problem not covered by James' argument is the implicit tyranny of the group that comes when the stress is not on truth in religion, but on the "religious values." These values tend to be the values of a particular group, and the result is that the group is deified. Thus there is nothing in the philosophy of James to deal with the problem of the totalitarian aspects of social groups. This very thing can be seen in many American communities where stress on the religious values has been followed by a suburban totalitarianism.

CHRISTIAN SELFLESSNESS

Another approach to the problem has been to say that the modern approach to personality and the stress on the self is nothing but the assertion of the Greek pride of life against the Christian stress on humility. This approach might quote Augustine's dictum on love, namely, that the love of God in the highest form implies the hate of self. Calvin himself has spoken of "suspended desire." We are not now interested in raising the historical problem of Calvin and his relation to Stoicism; but we are interested in those who have followed the ethics of selflessness and the insistence that the Christian must be purged of self, must not complain, but must accept the will of God for the direction of the events of life.

This group has generally argued from verses like Matthew 16:24: "let him deny himself and take up his cross," or Galatians 2:20: "I have been crucified with Christ; it is no longer I who live, but Christ who lives in me," or the δοῦλος Χριστοῦ of Paul, or the prayer of Jesus in Gethsemane: "Thy will be done." Some have taken Nygren's great work on love and insisted that any assertion of the will to live is the upward thrust of eros in its egocentricity. The interesting feature of this approach is that it has not only denied any validity to modern psychology, but has also to deal with the fact that the New Testament does not have the word "selflessness" or the Stoic ἀπάθεια in its vocabulary. Likewise the term αὐτάρκεια, a word in great favor

with the Stoics, was insignificant among the virtues listed
in the New Testament.

While this fact may not rule out the contention of those
who preach the ethic of selflessness as a Christian concept, it does demand that further consideration be given
to the biblical understanding of selfhood and selflessness.

CHRISTIAN MYSTICS

Another approach to the problem of selfhood is suggested by the Christian mystics. While those who preach
the ethic of selflessness speak of subordination to the will
of God, the Christian mystic stresses union with God. The
attraction of this position is the evidence of mystical language in the New Testament (as Deissmann would claim)
and the need for personal "experience."

One of the classical expressions of this point of view is
found in Wilhelm Herrmann's *The Communion of the
Christian With God:* "Without that experience (an inner
immediateness) of God all the rest . . . does not deserve
the name of religion."[2] Likewise the stress on sin as egocentricity would mean to the mystic that the chief effort of
the Christian must be to escape the ego and to find absorption in the divine. However, if the will and the ego are to
be limited in this way, problems outside the sphere of selfhood arise. As Friedrich Heiler has pointed out, the whole
prayer life of supplication, of thanksgiving, and of praise
are undermined in mysticism when self-will is rejected. In
addition, how does the mystic relate to the group? The corporate religious association which is essential for the religious life of the New Testament community is more or
less incomprehensible to the logic of mysticism.

MODERN CONSENSUS

In the analysis of the various viewpoints, the consensus
seems to be that the assertion of self implies that the God-

2W. Herrmann, *The Communion of the Christian With God* (London: Williams &
Norgate, 1913), p. 20.

man relationship cannot be taken seriously. To be truly religious means either to limit self-assertion or to be more concerned with an awareness of God than an awareness of self. To put it briefly, too much of selfhood can destroy the religious relationship of man with God.

There is, however, a break in this consensus. William James was not the only one to object to the so-called Christian stress on subordination to God's will or union with God as the core of Christian expression. The emphasis coming out of existential philosophy, psychology, and the whole social democratic movement in Western Europe also underscored the importance of man and the value of selfhood. Most other writers of the period followed the same general lines as James in stressing the value of ethics and the healthly life without so much concern with personal religion. Insofar as there was religious stress, it was on ethical religion. The later part of the nineteenth century and the early part of the twentieth witnessed numerous interpretations of this type. In regard to the problem before us, these writers assumed what the mystic and the preacher of selflessness assumed. They too held that an intense concentration on God and his will could very easily tend to reduce man's self-awareness. Thus, while they opposed the older pattern of a mystic life, or an ethic of selflessness, their assumption about the God-man relation was the same. They too conceived of the God-man relationship in mathematical terms. With such an outlook, they found it logical to assume that the more attention was paid to God the less would be paid to man. This was not in all cases held in a strictly logical way, but it still played its role, and the stress of the liberal outlook in that day was on the social aspect of Christianity.

We are to a great extent heirs to this outlook. If we strive for selfhood and the free expression of man, we instinctively suspect anyone who lays heavy emphasis on the God-man relationship. On the other hand, if we admire the Christian mystic or the preacher of selflessness, we tend to suspect the social gospel or an emphasis on the importance of selfhood. In the light of this unspoken assumption—the more of self the less of God, or the more of God the less of self—we must ask if this is the understanding of the Bible.

SELFHOOD AND THE BIBLE

What should cause us to wonder is the dual stress of the Bible, which speaks of God's sovereignty but also of man's freedom. If the Bible, and the New Testament in particular, lays equal stress on these two elements, then the biblical outlook may be proceeding on a completely different assumption from the one outlined above. What does the Bible say about selfhood as it pertains to the God-man relationship? Does the Bible think in the same mathematical terms as modern man? Does it assume that the more there is of self the less there is of God, and vice versa?

The answer to this problem is not a short one, for the Old and the New Testaments were written in an age which was to a large extent prepsychological. Therefore there is no explicit discussion on the problem of selfhood in the Bible. The only way to arrive at a conclusion is to see if the God-man relationship as it is described in the Bible is a different sort of religionship than mysticism, the ethic of selflessness, or psychology would allow. It may be helpful first to talk around the point and see what the Bible, especially the New Testament, says about such related concepts as selflessness, freedom, assertion, and communion with God, the Holy Spirit, and the church.

SELFLESSNESS

It is often contended that the New Testament speaks of selflessness, but this is seen to be a very hasty conclusion when subjected to scrutiny. The usage of words which are translated "self" is oftentimes deceptive. The New Testament was not written in the age of Freud. William Sanday in a small book entitled *Personality in Christ and Ourselves* has cautioned the reader in this way:

> In biblical times the idea of the self or person was not yet developed; the idea of "soul" had made great progress, and when a biblical writer wished to speak of himself, he spoke of his "soul." There is rather a play upon two senses in such passages as "whosoever would save his soul [ψυχὴν] shall lose it, and whosoever shall lose his soul for my sake and the gospel's shall save it" (Mark 8:35).[3]

Therefore, the use of certain proof passages in the New Testament to uphold the conception of selflessness can be very misleading. The passage that is often spoken of in this respect is Matthew 16:24: "let him deny himself and take up his cross." This passage does not necessarily mean the psychological denial of individuality or of selfhood in the sense of forgetting one's desires and emotions in an almost stoic αὐτάρκεια, or apathy. Nor does killing "the old man" necessarily have the connotation of psychological selflessness.

In Romans 7:9 is another concept: "I was once alive apart from the law, but when the commandment came, sin revived and I died." Paul speaks of a death that is very much like a loss of selfhood, but it is not a desirable state. In this context "the old man" with its sinful desires is something entirely different. To kill "the old man" is thus not to become selfless. The parable of the Prodigal Son speaks of self-awareness ("he came to himself") as a desirable trait, and insofar as the elder brother is brushed aside, the parable does not depict subordination to God and denial of joy (which the elder brother seems to have represented) as the most desirable relation of man to God. All of this is presented to caution against any easy

claim that the New Testament uniformly praises selflessness. It does not.

HUMILITY AND LOVE

Another contention worth testing is the claim that the
New Testament concept of humility and love implies selflessness. Many scholars would agree with Alan Richardson in his article on "Humility" in his *Theological Wordbook
of the Bible,* where he holds that Christianity "introduced
a new virtue—Christian humility—into the world." The
next step is to say that humility is the most Christlike attitude. Rightly understood this may be true, but there is
something subtly misleading about this contention. Those
sections of the church that have adopted this view have, like
Jerome, found it hard to account for the righteous indigna-
tion of the Apostle Paul.

I suggest that the New Testament does not praise humility as a virtue or end in itself. In criticizing asceticism Paul
condemns humility as an end in itself with the words:
"These have indeed an appearance of wisdom in promoting rigor of devotion and self-abasement [ταπεινοφροσύνη]
and serverity to the body, but they are of no value in check-
ing the indulgence of the flesh" (Col. 2:23). The Magnificat,
the prime example of humility to Richardson, contains in
addition the *unhumble* joy expressed by Mary—"For be-
hold, henceforth all generations will call me blessed." Humility in the sense of "holy indifference"[4] has no place in the
New Testament. The "Thy will be done" of Gethsemane is
not pure passivity, but what Heiler calls "prophetic prayer."

> The prayer of Jesus ... has been considered by all Chris-
> tian mystics to be the prototype of mystic resignation.
> And yet his [Jesus'] surrender to the will of the Father
> differs psychologically and fundamentally from Stoic or
> mystic resignation ... prophetic surrender is active and
> positive, there is no suppression of the desires ... it is
> the outcome of a psychic struggle and is won through the

4See F. Heiler, *Prayer* (London: Oxford University Press, 1932), p. 221.

discarge of emotion . . . it presupposes the simple expression of a concrete wish.[5]

As Leivestad put it in *Christ the Conqueror*, the temptation presupposes resistance to the tempter. Doing God's will involves assertion. As Christ challenged the Pharisees, he was at once too humble and too proud for the Jewish mentality. There is no solid claim that the New Testament concept of humility and love implies psychological selflessness.

When Nietzsche opposed Christ and Christians as weaklings, he was confusing the popular piety of his day with the piety of the New Testament. In the New Testament context, saying "Thy will be done" does not involve the loss of selfhood at all. The New Testament does not think of man relating himself to God in a vacuum of mystical piety, but always thinks of man relating himself to God in terms of the cosmic struggle with evil. The Christian does not subordinate himself to God's will, but rather acts as one who is carrying out God's will. Self-awareness is heightened because union of the will with the Father involves more personal assertion than a life not related to God, in the sense that the individual allied with God has taken up arms with God against evil. The New Testament also speaks of the implementation of the Christian who is fighting evil, and this also heightens self-awareness. Just how this is accomplished in the life of the Christian will be taken up later.

Because humility is not a virtue or an end in itself, there is little to support the contention that the New Testament concept of humility implies selflessness. The reverse seems to be true. The humble Christian in his fight against evil seems to have a heightened sense of his selfhood.

FREEDOM

It is well to heed the warning of Gabriel Marcel that freedom cannot be discussed by itself. If freedom is to be

---

[5]*Ibid.*, pp. 269 f.

linked with some type of autarchy, as we have in Nietzsche, and to an extent in Freud, then we must take the
position that the New Testament is not interested in freedom. While Nietsche's concept of freedom is most drastic,
it is not socially radical, for his freedom is something for
the few who can separate themselves from the mass. This
is the product of man's will, and only the strong man has
the right to be free in this sense of being beyond good and
evil.

The New Testament has a contrasting view of freedom.
It has a different starting point, for it is not man's will but
God's will that makes man free. This is also socially radical, for every man is forced into the position of freedom.
As Kierkegaard has pointed out, Christian freedom has
a dreadful aspect. The freedom which God gives is the
necessity of choice. Man is free in the sense that he must
choose between good and evil. This is not the natural freedom of man; it is the situation of man before a God who
is confronting him with the issue of his own life. This is
the horrible freedom of the Prodigal Son—the capacity
for self-destruction. This capacity is not something he has
of himself, but is part of his inheritance. Such freedom
produces self-awareness in the individual, and it involves
the dread of aloneness. Kierkegaard pictures man as
placed by God on the witness stand. This theological and
transcendent extension of the problem of freedom gives
it urgency in the message of the New Testament. In this
respect the whole romantic movement was correct in
stressing freedom, but they erred in tending to think of
it in individualistic terms as a human achievement. Thus
their stress on freedom, urgent as it is, is not as radical as
that of the New Testament. They could not say, as Kierkegaard did in a little essay entitled *God and Man*, that man's
greatest perfection is his need of God.

The fact is that the God-man relationship in the New
Testament is not thought of as absorption or subordina-

tion. Whether or not one likes the terminology of Tillich in all respects, one cannot deny the major thrust of his words on "reconciliation with God" involving "reconciliation with self."[6] The Damascus-road experience of Paul is not an example of a mystical experience of being filled with the love of God. While many interpreters have taken this view, the place at which Paul was met by God was not the state of ecstasy, but of sin. That God meets the Christian here, at the point of sin, means that the Christian so confronted will have a greater self-awareness, for this is not just the acceptance of sinfulness in general, as an article of belief. The confrontation by God results in the awareness of specific sins in the individuals who are confronted. Thus Paul learned that he could no longer persecute the church because this was a grave sin. The result was a union with the risen Christ. This is quite a contrast to the mystic union with God.

As Heiler has pointed out, the mystic finds little reason to ask for forgiveness. This is but another way of saying that the mystic has little use for the concept of individuality or selfhood in this sense. In answer to William James, the New Testament's radical understanding of freedom may be the reason why the Christian religion has more spiritual autobiographies than any other religion.

SERVICE AND CHARISMA

In the discussion of the conception of subordination it was maintained that assertion is part of the Christian's acceptance of God's will. This contention might be objected to as being a far cry from true selfhood. Those oriented in some schools of modern psychology might hold that when the New Testament speaks of service it slips from the high plane of forgiveness to the subpersonal plane of compulsion. Similarly Nygren and some other theologians, insisting that agape as described by Paul is

---

6P. Tillich, *The New Being* (New York: Charles Scribner's Sons, 1956), p. 21.

spontaneous, feel that the New Testament imperatives to love are contradictory.

It is quite obvious to say that God heightens the self-awareness of man when he confronts him at the point of sin. It is not so clear just what the precise relationship is between service to God and selfhood. When Paul argues that man is free and that God intended this freedom to be used for service, it seems as though Paul is caught in a contradiction. The contradiction is more logical than psychological, however. As Karen Horney has said, "The love of neighbor involves self-love." In this sense modern psychology and Paul's argument in Galatians are very close in basic outlook. The danger in the definition of Karen Horney is that a superficial interpretation of it tends to turn love of neighbor into a sort of rationalist self-interest. Whether it is from a pesudo-Freudian outlook or from the materialism of our times, there is a general antipathy toward the need for struggle and even suffering in the life of service.

It is at this point of avoiding suffering and sacrifice that the modern-day preacher of the ethic of selflessness makes his clearest plea. His cultural criticism is that man has become a seeker after the pleasure of life. He links this pursuit of happiness with modern man's quest for selfhood and concludes that his goal is wrong, and preaches that man is to deny himself. What this position overlooks in stressing the need for selflessness is the connection which the New Testament makes between selfhood and service. As Paul points out in the thirteenth chapter of First Corinthians, service to the neighbor without the proper motivation is worthless. When Luther held that the unjustified man could not do good works he was saying that man who had not found his selfhood in being justified before God was not able to serve his fellow man. The New Testament in like manner could not think of service which would be selfless, but could only speak of a service which had selfhood as its basis.

In addition to this, Paul speaks about the relation between service and suffering in a unique way. The service of a Christian does involve suffering, but not only suffering. If service involved only suffering, then man would be crushed by his task, and this is not the case. The *charismata*, the gifts of the Spirit, are given at the point of stress to the man in the service of his Lord. Thus, in Paul, the term δοῦλος κυρίου means more than servant in the lowly sense. Paul was a servant of the Lord. This did not overlook the ennobling aspect of service. The gifts of teaching, preaching, healing, etc., are given to the man in the redemptive relationship with his fellow man. Paul says, "But we have this treasure in earthen vessels, to show that the transcendent power belongs to God and not to us. We are afflicted in every way, but not crushed; perplexed, but not driven to despair; persecuted, but not forsaken; struck down, but not destroyed." The disciples in their first mission, in which they carried nothing, were given the ἐξουσία. The consolation of Jesus is that in the terrifying work of spreading the Gospel to the world, he will be present. In persecution he will counteract the terror of the accused with the gift of speech, etc. This is a far cry from a plea to give up self in service. It presupposes that the man who serves has selfhood, and it promises that at the point where his service leads him to doubt, suffering, and persecution he will be strengthened and enabled to experience his true selfhood.

THE SELF AND THE CORPORATE

The preceding study has shown that the New Testament does not conceive of the God-man relationship in terms of a mystic absorption of the self in God or a stoic subordination of the self to the will of God. Little has been said about the bearing which the relation of the Christian to the church has upon the problem of selfhood.

Such a question must be asked because it often happens in practice that the church is an antipersonal factor in society. Because of this, there have been many critics of the church and of "togetherness" in general. Nietzsche's quest for selfhood is perhaps more of a pattern for modern man than many of us would like to admit. He praised the hermit type of existence in his book *Thus Spake Zarathustra*: "Having attained the age of thirty, Zarathustra left his home and the lake of his home and went into the mountains. Then he rejoiced in his spirit and in his loneliness, and for ten years did not grow weary of it."[7] Mystics also see little value in the church, and the nineteenth century has many examples of an attitude of disregard for the church and the church fellowship. In the words of Wilhelm Herrmann "we outgrow our dependence on our surroundings."[8]

Such a position as Herrmann's is no longer as easily held, because the central aspect of the preaching of Jesus is now recognized to be the declaration that the kingdom of God was at hand. Jesus is no longer portrayed as the ethical teacher who had no intention of establishing a group of believers. The New Testament does not say that one is a Christian first and only then a member of a church. If selfhood is thought of in terms of an individualistic assertion that separates one from the corporate religious body or minimizes its importance, then the New Testament stops short of a concern for selfhood in the sociological dimension.

However, while the New Testament does stress the corporate life of the believers, it does not do so in such a way as to limit its high valuation of selfhood. In the New Testament conception of corporate religious life there are two factors which at the same time stress selfhood.

---

[7]F. Nietzsche *Thus Spake Zarathustra* (New York: The Macmillan Company, 1906), p. 1.

[8]See *The Communion of a Christian With God*, p. 118.

The first of these factors is the insistence that within the congregation there is variety. This variety is thought of as essential. Paul's whole discussion in First Corinthians stresses that each member of the body of Christ has a function, and that for this reason uniformity would be a denial of the body of Christ. (See 1 Cor. 12:12-19.)

The second factor is Paul's conception of the body of Christ, which enhances selfhood in a paradoxical way in which God honors the members by "giving the greater honor to the inferior part" (1 Cor. 12:24). This characteristic is possible only with the presence of the risen Christ in his body, the church. In the body of Christ each Christian is given a task, but it is not simply that he is chosen for his natural qualifications. That would not enhance selfhood. What does enhance selfhood is that in addition to natural qualifications each is divinely equipped for his special task. The result is that the church, because of the divine activity of the Spirit, paradoxically heightens the selfhood of those who relate themselves to this group.

CONCLUSION

This presentation does not exhaust the consideration of selfhood, but on the basis of the foregoing discussion some suggestions can be made. There are two basic ways to look at selfhood: mathematically and organically.

The mathematical way of looking at the relation of the self to the group and to God would be to say that the less there is of the group or of God, the more there is of the self, and the more there is of self, the less there is of the religious group and of God. As has been pointed out, this seems to be the attitude of many non-Christian observers of Christianity, and also of Christian mystics and preachers of the ethic of selflessness. The latter two groups seek to honor God by suppressing the self in one way or the other. This is not a totally different view from that of the pragmatist who says that a healthy religion does not concern itself with the God-man relationship so much as with religious values.

Against this consensus we have placed the viewpoint of the New Testament. The New Testament recognizes the native wisdom of the above statements, yet it points to a radically personal God, to a church as the body of Christ, and to the world as the place of God's activity. This study has been directed to showing that the New Testament does not think of selfhood in the mathematical way of modern ethics, of Christian self-denial, or of Christian mysticism, but that it has an organic view instead. By speaking of an organic view I mean to use the analogy of the plant. As the root of the plant gets bigger, so does the branch. The concentration of a Christian on God does not mean that he plays down his selfhood. In the view of the New Testament the reverse is true. As the Christian attaches himself to his God, to his church, and relates himself to this world, he finds in this engagement his own selfhood. This is true because the New Testament does not view selfhood as a human achievement but as a product of God's dealing with men. Because God is personal he forces man into a dialogue, and calls man to his true selfhood in freedom, in service, and in his church.

The hope of this study is that selfhood will not be thought of in the purely mathematical way that is so natural for us all, but that the New Testament view, with its organic way of looking at the problem, will be given its chance to impress upon us the depth of its insights in this most important aspect of man's existence.

VII

Emotional Health and Its Relation to Christian Experience

When a person becomes a Christian, is it apparent in his personality?

This question may be asked in other ways. For example, it could be phrased: "What are the emotional and behavioral characteristics of the Christian experience?" Or, "What emotional resources result from one's Christian faith?" In the context of this book, the question may be stated: "What is the relationship between emotional health and Christian experience?"

It is the opinion of the author that the emotional and personality benefits often promised from being a Christian are generally overrated. Careful observation rather indicates that one's Christian faith plays a relatively minor role among the many factors that influence the degree of one's emotional maturity. It will be the purpose of this essay to demonstrate how the resources of Christianity, and more particularly the resources of the Christian community, can be used at least to a moderate degree to improve the mental health of Christians. But the thesis here will be that Protestantism generally has promised too much about emotional gains resulting from Christian faith.

The traditional answers to the question raised by this

DR. KILDAHL is a psychologist at the Lutheran Medical Center, Brooklyn, New York.

143

paper range from a conviction that belief in God is down-
right destructive of emotional health and maturity to the
view that a Christian experience totally remakes the personality, resolves emotional conflicts, produces mental health,
and in some cases results in a sinless perfectionism.

WHAT IS EMOTIONAL HEALTH?

Does one's Christian faith contribute to his emotional
health?

A preliminary matter, then, is a description of what is
meant by good emotional health. One of the most popular
definitions is this: Good emotional health is the ability to
receive and to give love and to take responsibility. The
absence of any of the three elements would indicate a serious shortcoming in a person's emotional maturity.

The National Association for Mental Health[1] has noted
three characteristics of people with good mental health:
(1) They feel comfortable about themselves. (2) They feel
right about other people. (3) They are able to meet the
demands of life. Such people are not overwhelmed by any
of their emotions—by their fears, anger, love, jealousy,
guilt, or worries. They have personal relationships that are
lasting, and they neither push people around nor allow themselves to be pushed around. They shape their environment
whenever possible and adjust to it whenever necessary.

Finally, a third description of good emotional health is
that offered by Rollo May,[2] a psychoanalyst. For him, good
adjustment involves (1) the individual's progressive realization of his own unique capacities, and, at the same time, (2)
his increasing sense of community with his fellow men. He
is healthy to the extent that he can expand the development
of his own powers while also releasing the fears which have
kept him from close communication with other people.

In the diagnosis of emotional disorders there are three

1*Mental Health Is One, Two, Three* (New York: The National Association for
Mental Health, 1951).
2Rollo May, *The Meaning of Anxiety* (New York: The Ronald Press Co., 1950).

places to look for possible difficulties: a person's *thought,* his *mood,* and his *behavior.* The emotionally healthy person shows no marked deviation in any of these three areas.

In this essay, when mental or emotional health and maturity are mentioned, the descriptions noted above will be the context of those phrases.

The Protestant church has generally maintained that Christian faith contributes to emotional health and maturity. Much of Protestant preaching distinctly implies that mental health accrues from being a Christian. Sunday after Sunday most Protestants hear that they will *feel better* if they put their trust in the Lord, that their unhappiness is in some way related to unbelief, and that somehow the righteous ones are also the mature ones. I have personally never met a minister who, when asked about it, would claim such a one-to-one relationship between faith and emotional health. Yet, dozens of Christians have told me that this is precisely what they have learned from hundreds of sermons; namely, that if they would only believe, their fears and tensions would be quieted.

Three segments of Protestantism will be described below, grouped according to their emphasis and viewpoint regarding the interrelationship of faith and emotional health. As will be seen, they vary in their method of promoting such emotional health. They also vary according to the degree of such health they believe will accrue from religious faith. The survey of these three segments of Protestantism will serve as a background and context for the author's own later comments and suggestions concerning how the church can and cannot promote better mental health.

THREE CHRISTIAN APPROACHES

There are three groups within the Christian framework that claim that their approach to the Christian faith materially betters one's mental health. First, there is the part of the church that strives for a sudden and dramatic religious conversion, believing that personality changes and emotional integration thus take place. At present, Billy Graham is a leading spokesman for this group. Second, there is the part of the church that is described as the positive-thinking school of thought, closely identified with the name of Norman Vincent Peale. Third, we have the more traditional approach of the bulk of the middle of Protestantism, which says that through the Means of Grace, the Word and the Sacraments there takes place a gradual sanctification of one's life. These three emphases overlap considerably and are classified in this way only for purposes of easier explanation. There is a possible fourth general category, namely, that of Christian mysticism. But its influence today is more narrow than that of the other three, and its methods will not be evaluated here.

We shall briefly examine these three religious approaches to mental health problems in order to see how they "work" and by what means they do or do not promote emotional integration.

DRAMATIC RELIGIOUS CONVERSIONS. A sudden and dramatic religious conversion has been described as an experience that seems to the subject to include: first, a conviction marked by a sense of guilt and unworthiness; second, a crisis in which a definite change of attitude is effected, sometimes by positive striving and in other cases by a "letting go"; and third, a relaxation in which the person feels flooded with joy, peace, and happiness.[3]

Billy Graham describes the results of conversion as follows:

> When you are born again, several results will follow:
> First, it will increase your vision and understanding.
> Your whole mental process is changed. . . . The ego has
> been dethroned.
> Second, your heart undergoes a revolution. Your affections
> have undergone a radical change. Your heart beats with
> new compassion for those around you. Third, your will
> undergoes a tremendous change. Your motivations are

---
[3]G. A. Coe, *The Psychology of Religion* (Chicago: University of Chicago Press, 1916).

changed. . . . There were falsehoods and hypocrisies in
many of your thoughts, words, and deeds. That is now all
changed. Your very nature has changed.[4]

One convert described his own experience in this way:

> I was converted in my own bedroom. . . . The stillness was
> very marvelous, and I felt supremely happy. . . . The Spir-
> it of God showed me ineffable love. . . . I committed my-
> self to Him. . . . In such surrender lies the secret of a
> holy life. . . . With every known sin, the deliverance in
> each case was permanent and complete. I have had no
> temptation since conversion. Since I gave up to God all
> ownership in my own life, he has guided me in a thousand
> ways, and has opened my path in a way almost incredible
> to those who do not enjoy the blessing of truly surren-
> dered life.[5]

How can such results be accounted for? It is well to remember that conversions are rather widespread psychological phenomena, occurring not only within the Christian
church but in non-Christian situations as well. They can
occur in relation to other beliefs, such as Communism, or
other religions. Or there can be equally striking changes
from a religious to an irreligious state. The psychological
results may be the same: an abrupt change in the direction
of one's life, and accompanying feelings of great peace, harmony, and contentment. William James, for example, has
described many different cultural and ideological effects in
which conversions occur—and the psychological or emotional effects are astonishingly similar, regardless of what
the context was in which those various conversions occurred.
Salzman,[6] a psychoanalyst, notes that conversions occur in
the realms of religious, moral, political, ethical, and esthetic
views. Salzman points out that Whittaker Chambers in his
book *Witness* gives a good description of the close relationship between political and religious conversions.

4Billy Graham, *Peace With God* (Garden City, N.Y.: Doubleday and Co., 1956).
5Wm. James, *The Varieties of Religious Experience* (New York: The Modern
Library, Copyright 1902).
6L. Salzman, "The Psychology of Religious and Ideological Conversions, *Psychiatry*
(1953), *16*, pp. 183-87.

It is important also to note that conversions may or may not be conducive to better emotional integration. Dramatic religious coversions are invariably marked by great conflict. Boisen, a hospital chaplain, makes the point that:

> Pathological experiences are frequently attended by religious concern, and religious experience by pathological features. This is explained by the fact that both may be attempts to solve some difficult and vital problem. When the outcome is constructive, we are likely to recognize it as a religious experience. When it is destructive or inconclusive, we call it "mental disorder." The outcome of an acute disturbance is dependent upon the assets and liabilities which the individual brings to the crisis experience . . . . and his previous preparation.[7]

Salzman[6] has noted six post-conversion characteristics of what he calls regressive conversions:

> 1) The convert has an exaggerated, irrational intensity of belief. 2) The convert is concerned more with form and doctrine than with the greater principle of the new belief. 3) His attitude toward his previous belief is one of contempt, hatred, and denial, and he rejects the possibility that there might be any truth in it. 4) He is intolerant toward all deviates, with frequent acting out by denouncing and endangering previous friends and associates. 5) He shows a crusading zeal and a need to involve others by seeking new converts. 6) He engages in masochistic and sadistic activities, displaying a need for martyrdom and self-punishment.

Weininger, another psychoanalyst, says that the main problem of a person who is about to have a religious conversion is that he is having great difficulty in adjusting to a group. The sense of social failure is prominent, and the conversion offers a new and better adaptation to having a relationship with people. Thereby, and for the time being, the sense of isolation disappears. Such a person feels that he has been living wrongly and that there is an opposite ideal to which he would like to conform.

7Anton T. Boisen, *Religion in Crisis and Custom* (New York: Harper & Brothers, 1955).

When a person in inner conflict becomes exhausted with his struggle, or when he reaches the point where he has sunk to a very low feeling of self-esteem, feels utterly worthless and helpless, and thereby gives up the will power struggle, a religious conversion experience may take place.[8]

Weininger then adds that when such a person meets someone else who shows a genuine interest in him, a radical change occurs. The second person shows that he does not find the person unacceptable, that there can be a solution to his problem, that he need not struggle fruitlessly, and that he can be helped by a religious approach. "Religious conversions are brought about through the intervention and acceptance by another person. The other person acts as a catalyst."[8] A book alone, unless that book was suggested by an interested *person,* would probably not be sufficient stimulus to precipitate a conversion. Being accepted by the other person, guilt and all, relieves the anxiety sufficiently to enable the compulsive struggle to decrease; and as the struggle stops, the remaining anxiety subsides. The acceptance by the catalyst person makes possible the cessation of the struggle.

This brief survey of some of the psychological factors in conversion is intended to point up the complexity of the phenomenon: conversion occurs in other realms than the religious; it may or may not bring about better emotional integration; it is probably most often a consequence of previous social isolation and may be an attempt to achieve closer contact with people.[9]

There are certain definite methods by which an atmosphere conducive to conversions can be created. Evangelists know very well what these conditions are. But so also have

---

[8]Benjamin Weininger, "The Interpersonal Factor in Religious Experience." *Psychoanalysis* (1955), *3,* pp. 27-44.

[9]This evaluation is not meant to imply that conversion is either good or bad. It is not the purpose of this paper to enter into how or whether this may be the Spirit of God at work, nor to pass any other theological judgment on the phenomenon of conversion. This is simply a *psychological* attempt to explain one small part of a person's behavior—and to show how this bit of behavior may be explained on *psychological* bases.

all leaders of mass movements known what these methods are. There is apparently nothing psychologically unique in revival movements. There is no unique emotional quality in religious experiences wrought at the hands of an evangelist. Those same experiences can be produced by other types of leaders using similar methods. It is possible to have sudden and dramatic "religious" conversions to vegetarianism, nazism, socialism, or agnosticism.[10] Every observable and known psychological quality is identical. These conversions may or may not confer the same integration of personality, depending on the conflicts with which the subject wrestled at the time.

Some denominational groups put much *greater* stress on sudden conversions, and they make *greater* efforts to secure them. Consequently they have *greater* success statistically.

Who is converted by such methods? It has long been known that certain personality types are more susceptible to sudden conversions than others.[11] It is highly unlikely that persons of certain personality types could ever experience a dramatic conversion. For other types, the chances are that if they are religious at all and are exposed to revivalistic methods, they will have a dramatic conversion. Previous research by the author has indicated that sudden religious converts are, on the average, less intelligent and more hysteric than are equated persons of a gradual religious development.[12]

Sudden conversions will probably always occur, as indeed they have done for at least twenty centuries. There is still

10An intriguing, but perhaps somewhat impious, experiment would be to conduct as well organized a campaign as, for example, Billy Graham's—only on behalf of vegetarianism. Use the same methods and strategy, same approach, same publicity; attract the same large crowds; use as personable a speaker. I wonder if the percentage of converts would be the same as Graham's.

11Much has been written on what personality types are the most likely candidates for sudden religious conversions. The three most complete such descriptions will be found in E. Starbuck, *The Psychology of Religion* (New York: Scribner's, 1912) ; G. Coe, *The Spiritual Life* (New York: Abingdon, 1900) ; and ᴇ. Clark, *The Psychology of Religious Awakening* (New York: Macmillan, 1929). Sigmund Freud has also described the emotional factors in religious conversion: "A Religious Experience," *Collected Papers* (London: Hogarth Press, 1950), V.

12John P. Kildahl, *Personality Correlates of Sudden Religious Converts Contrasted with Persons of a Gradual Religious Development*, unpublished Ph.D. thesis, New York University, 1957.

an issue as to whether or not this type of experience should be fostered. There are certainly definite techniques by which such conversions can be brought about. Should the church use such methods? May such techniques not be simply ways of manipulating human emotions so as to bring about a certain end?

There is no available evidence that such conversion experiences are any more integrating, longer lasting, or more effective than a gradual approach. There do seem to be some harmful side effects in some sudden converts, particularly in the sociological aspects of religious conversion. A person not only gets converted to a certain faith, he usually also is converted to certain cultural mores. This can be upsetting because it can be a disintegrating influence. It often means a complete change of clothes, vocation, leisure time activities, friends, etc. It is my experience in doing psychotherapy with some sudden converts that they are still left with many unresolved conflicts. They are ill-prepared to handle these conflicts because the tacit assumption of their group was that conversion would solve all their problems. It seems certain, for example, that Billy Graham knows better than to expect such postconversion freedom from problems. But he certainly does not prepare his listeners adequately to understand that such will invariably be the case. The result is that the new convert feels either let down or that he is an unworthy follower of his new way of life.

To conclude this section on conversion: Sudden converts tend, on the average, to fall into a certain personality type, i.e., the hysteric type. Hysterics are usually quite emotionally labile and subject to mood swings. They are more easily dominated by emotions than by intellectual efforts. Naïvete and moralism are particularly evident. In contrast to this type of approach to life, the church today rather needs people who are critical, reflective, and persistent thinkers. Uncritical, naïve acceptance of whole theological and social systems is hardly what this age demands—but it is this approach which the sudden convert usually adopts. To the extent that sudden conversions place a final stamp of approval on the denomination in which they occurred, they are depriving the convert of the impetus to examine and question his religious experiences. It would seem likely that a slower, more reasoned approach to one's religious faith provides a person with better equipment to deal with the questions that inevitably must occur to the believer. That person is ill-equipped who tends not to reflect on his beliefs. Any religious experiences which can help the believer to examine his beliefs should be encouraged. For this reason, the sudden and dramatic religious conversion falls short of optimally promoting mental or emotional growth.

THE POSITIVE-THINKING APPROACH. The essentials of the Peale system for promoting emotional health have been used for some centuries. Basically, it consists in a person's trying to think about only optimistic, successful, and positive ideas and situations. At the same time, one should try to avoid any thought of negativism, defeatism, or unhappiness. The Rev. Dr. Peale also includes God in this system and maintains that one should think optimistically about what God can do in one's life. It should be stated, however, that inclusion of thoughts about God is not invariably necessary to the success of this method or system of mental health. In a number of Dr. Peale's formulas God is not mentioned.

Peale's position is well known. In his writings he has outlined methods for using one's Christian faith so that life will be full of joy, satisfaction, happiness, and well-being. A brief quotation will refresh the reader's memory:

> If you read this book thoughtfully . . . and practice the principles and formulas . . . you can experience an amazing improvement within yourself. Your relations with other people will improve. You will become more popular . . . you will enjoy a delightful new sense of well-being . . . and experience a new and keen pleasure in living. You will become a person of greater usefulness and will wield an expanded usefulness. . . . I need not point out

that the powerful principles contained herein are not my invention but are given to us by the greatest Teacher who ever lived and still lives. This book teaches applied Christianity; a simple yet scientific system of practical techniques of successful living that works.[13]

This system often works, i.e., it helps people feel better. There can be no doubt of this. There is little question that the testimonies recorded by Dr. Peale's followers are true statements of what actually happened in their lives. I am personally acquainted with persons who seem to have been helped by these methods.

As a general rule, it is helpful for anyone to focus primaridly through praise than as a result of criticism. Therefore, tifically demonstrable fact that behavior changes more rapidly through praise than as a result of criticism. Therefore, if we make some allowance for Dr. Peale's natural exuberance in promulgating his own doctrine (i.e., the system), and fit the whole thing into the context of what we know about mental illness and health, then we have a useful tool which truly can help individuals lead more satisfying and constructive lives.

There should be an appendix, however, to all Dr. Peale's writings. This is what I believe the appendix should include: The positive-thinking approach to mental health *cannot* and *will not* work in every person. Nor will it bring successful results to any one person under all circumstances. While it can be helpful as a *general* rule in the *average* person in *many* circumstances, it simply is not the answer in countless other situations. There is, in fact, a considerable danger in proclaiming its usefulness under all conditions.

As I have seen people helped by the Peale system, so I have also seen people harmed by it. For example, when a person has conscientiously tried always to think positively, but has been unable to do so with the results promised by Dr. Peale, that person usually feels worse off than before. And

---

[13]Norman Vincent Peale, *The Power of Positive Thinking* (New York: Prentice-Hall, 1952).

he generally blames himself (for being so sick, so bad, so hopeless, having too little faith, etc.) for not being able to achieve the promised results of happiness, usefulness, and buoyance. Rather than blaming the method, such a person generally blames himself—which has the effect of another knock on the head.

It is my opinion that Dr. Peale himself realizes the deleterious effect on a person when the method fails, or when another approach would be more appropriate. Occasionally Dr. Peale implies as much in his writings. Yet this apparently does not get across to enough of his readers, with the consequence that they are even more self-derogating than before.

The point is that the Peale method does not work, and no claims for its workability should be made, under many conditions of life. It works best in healthy, normal people. For them, the use of positive thinking can increase their effectiveness. For people who are only moderately depressed or anxious, there can also be some help through this method. However, it should also be said that there is much positive good in *negative* thinking.

No attempt should be made to use the Peale system with seriously upset people. Such people must get at the *cause* of their problems and not deal only with the symptoms. The Peale approach pays little or no heed to the underlying causes of emotional distress, namely, the various emotional conflicts which are often unconscious. These conflicts are unconscious because the mechanism of repression is operating to push painful conflicts out of awareness. There can be no lasting, effective change unless the person has resolved those problems which made him feel upset. While thinking about optimistic possibilities may help temporarily, genuine changes occur only when one has self-understanding. Any system which focuses on the *symptoms* and which fails to deal with the *causes* of behavior can only be a palliative and not a remedy.

In the Peale system occasional references are made to the importance of the cause of one's upset. But, by and large, the system is concerned only with what lies on the surface, i.e., one's outward behavior. This is the main reason for its superficiality; there is not enough stress put on how and why a person became anxious or tense or depressed. Without such insight, there is little chance of lasting change. To use an analogy from the realm of physical illness, the positive-thinking approach may have the effect of an aspirin but can never do the work of an antibiotic.

THE MIDDLE PROTESTANT APPROACH. The approach of the bulk of Protestantism is neither to strive for a sudden religious conversion on the one hand, nor to promise the dramatic gains in personality growth described by the positive-thinking school, on the other.

There are many different shades of emphasis, of course, depending on the background, training, and personality of the preacher or theologian. But for purposes of summary here, it may be said that this group puts *relatively* little emphasis on the personality gains resulting from the Christian faith. It would be unlikely that such words as were quoted from either Graham or Peale would be used today by a preacher in the average Lutheran, Presbyterian, Episcopal, or Methodist congregation.

The traditional Lutheran approach is that there is no easy way toward sanctification, i.e., toward holiness or Christ-likeness. Men are, all their lives, plagued by two natures—good and evil. And there is no time when one part is eliminated and the other part fully achieved. This being the case, it follows that there can be no facile promises made about easy relief from unwanted moods or actions.

The Christian life is portrayed by St. Paul as a race, a struggle, and a conflict. "Not that I have already obtained . . . ," he wrote. On the other hand, stupendous goals were urged upon Christ's followers. "You, therefore, must be perfect." And the promises were equally great: "If any one is in Christ, he is a new creation."

Thus there is this continuing tension. It is tension between what is expected of the Christian, what he is promised, and what he is able to do. It is continuing because it is literally true that no one does attain to the state of being without sin or of loving with perfect maturity. St. John, in his First Epistle, acknowledges the continuing conflict by these two statements: "If we say we have no sin, we deceive ourselves," and "No one born of God commits sin."

The Christian faith does not abolish anxiety, nor does it heal emotional disorders. Personality maladjustments continue beyond forgiveness. Neurotic practices become intertwined with religious practices.

It is the consensus of expert psychological opinion today that there is no one who is ideally mature. Rather, everyone has some unreasonable worries and unfounded fears, or inferiority feelings or a bad disposition. Two psychiatrists summarize this view. Dr. Jules Coleman says, "Almost everybody—far from being happy—is actually unhappy most of the time." And Dr. Erich Lindemann says that religious thinkers and philosophers have always taken account of "the misery and failure in life" and have made no claim of "everything being solvable in an optimistic way." Dr. Elaine Cumming, a sociologist, adds, "Unhappiness is man's inheritance; all of us are bound to be sad and grief-stricken at times. The capacity to feel sad is perhaps just the other side of the capacity to feel happy. So the most useful thing we can teach is that life is complex and difficult—and the more roses you seek, the more likely you are to fall upon thorns."[14]

All this is consonant with good Christian teaching. It follows consistently from the Christian doctrine of man; namely, that man is evil, in the sense that he does not keep

---

[14]All three of the previous quotations are taken from the *Life* magazine article of August 8, 1960, by Ernest Havemann entitled "Who's Normal? Nobody, but We All Keep Trying."

the moral law perfectly, simultaneously with an immense capacity for good. As Dr. Orville S. Walters, a psychiatrist, writes:

> Among the diverse and conflicting doctrines of man, none explains as much as the Christian view. In contrast to the instinctual emphasis of Freud who saw man as primarily biological, or of the neo-Freudians who see man as primarily social, the Christian doctrine of man acknowledges that he is these and more. The Christian approach offers a synoptic view of man presenting him as a spiritual being with elements in his nature that respond to transcendental reality. Humanistic views that emphasize primarily man's good and the pessimistic Freudian articles of faith are exceeded in the broader, more realistic Christian doctrine that sees, beyond man's basic evil, his limitless potential for good through divine redemption and grace. In marked contrast to the freshly minted theories of human nature, the Christian doctrine enjoys a coherence and maturity that has withstood centuries of the severest attack and criticism without essential change.[15]

Thus it is that most Protestants today recognize both the need to strive toward emotional maturity and the fact that such an ideal state is unattainable. This is why it is unrealistic to preach sermons which promise relief from all emotional suffering—such a state being unattainable, either by Christian or non-Christian. To make such promises is therefore ill-considered. By taking a more realistic approach, the church will avoid making promises to Christians which cannot possibly be fulfilled.

WHAT SHOULD THE CHURCH CLAIM?

Should Christians make the claim that Christian belief materially reduces nervous tension? It is the opinion of this author that much harm has been done by the widespread and unreflective statements of Christian leaders on this matter. The facts of the situation appear to be that Chris-

---

15Orville S. Walters, "The Psychiatrist and Christian Faith," *The Christian Century*, LXXVII, July 20, 1960, pp. 847-49.

tian faith and emotional integration are not *causally* related. That is, a person does not *necessarily* become more emotionally healthy because he becomes a believer in Christ. Emotional maturity *may* increase in some such cases; in others it may not.

One's Christian faith and one's emotional health may be considered as being in two different dimensions—which do not necessarily intersect. Since these two dimensions do not necessarily intersect, it is possible that one's faith may not influence his emotional health and vice versa.

For our purposes here, let us very briefly describe Christianity as involving primarily the Word (Logos) of and about God. The mental health of a person, on the other hand, depends on the number and degree of his emotional conflicts and on how well or how poorly he handles these conflicts. In the light of these descriptions of Christianity and of mental health, it can be seen that it is possible that they may not influence each other. To quote Professor David Roberts:

> We have only to think of the familiar situation in which a pastor and parishioner (who may agree with each other on doctrinal questions) find that a sincere, conscious acceptance of Christian belief does not suffice to remove the psychological blockages and moral failures which are destroying the happiness and perhaps even the sanity of the latter.[16]

After listening to many emotionally troubled Christians, the author has developed a conviction that much harm has come from the church's claim that it provides, or at least successfully promotes, emotional integration. Most Christians who seek psychotherapy[17] do so with at least some guilt feelings about their need for psychotherapy. They have

---

16David E. Roberts, "Health from the Standpoint of the Christian Faith," in *The Church and Mental Health*, Paul B. Maves, ed. (New York: Chas. Scribner's Sons, 1953).

17Psychotherapy may be defined as "a form of treatment for problems of an emotional nature in which a trained person deliberately establishes a professional relationship with a patient with the object of removing, modifying or retarding existing symptoms, of mediating disturbed patterns of behavior, and of prompting positive personality growth and development." Lewis R. Wolberg, *The Technique of Psychotherapy* (New York: Grune and Stratton, 1954).

somewhere acquired the belief that a good Christian ought not need the help of a psychotherapist. Such Christians are ashamed of themselves for having emotional problems. They feel that their problems must indicate that they do not *believe* strongly enough, and that therefore they must be poor Christians. Consequently, they suffer even more; first, because they have an emotional problem, and second, because they feel good Christians should not have such problems. Thus they may be even more self-derogating than a non-Christian with the identical problem.

Again, the preacher may rightly declare that he has never claimed that the Christian experience eliminates the possibility of emotional troubles. Nevertheless, the implication drawn by Christian after Christian is that if his faith is sound, then he will be emotionally sound also. Clinical experience indicates that this is simply not the case (unless one can engage in semantic tricks and say, after the fact, about a mentally ill person, "Well, apparently he didn't really[18] believe or he wouldn't have become ill"). Mental hospitals, as well as psychotherapists' waiting rooms contain their fair share of Christian believers. It seems impossible to be intellectually honest and still maintain that there is some imperfection in these persons' faith which accounts for their lack of immunity to emotional upsets. As the rain falls on the just and on the unjust, so also emotional problems affect the Christian and the non-Christian.

I could not do better at this point than to quote Karl Stern,[19] who writes:

> Even if overt anxiety has increased tremendously in our time, as it seems to have, it is dangerously fallacious to link this up with the question of the person within the order of Grace. . . . One can show many atheists who have never known a sleepless night or a dark hour, as against saintly people of the most intense mystic life who are torn by the temptation of despair. . . . It is true that

18Someone has called this "adverbial theology."
19Karl Stern, *The Third Revolution* (New York: Harcourt, Brace and Co., 1954).

Christ said to His disciples when they were afraid: 'Oh ye of little faith.' But He Himself knew the agony of the darkest night.

And Stern adds this cogent point:

Apart from the fallacy of the pat formula and the easy spiritual recipe, there is another fallacy. It is more hidden. When we say about the neurotic sufferer, "If he only had more faith . . .," we ourselves fall into the danger of Pharisaism. We are tempted to say, or we feel it without quite realizing it: "Look at me, I believe and I have no anxiety. I thank you, God, that you have not made me like those."

When the church tacitly or explicitly implies that relief from anxiety comes through faith, most Christians are done a disservice. In most cases the Christian then blames himself. In other cases the believer blames his church for making unjustified claims. In either case, both the Christian and his church suffer because someone made claims for the relief of emotional distress by *means* of the Christian faith. Such relief very often does not come—regardless of how sincere the Christian is in his belief.

FACTORS WHICH PROMOTE EMOTIONAL HEALTH

What are those factors which promote sound emotional health? If there is not evidence that one's Christian faith and one's emotional health are causally related, what then are the causes of good emotional health?

There are several factors which are essential to good emotional integration. They are the *sine qua non* of mental health. Although the list of factors may vary somewhat, most psychologists agree on the following five elements. Psychologists believe that these basic needs have been experimentally and empirically validated. They must all be present in a person if he is to measure up to the descriptions of the best mental health noted above.

First, a person needs a feeling of self-esteem and moral worth.

Second, a person needs to feel that his own strength is relatively equal to the strength of his environment, i.e., that he can cope with his world.

Third, a person needs to feel that his relationships with people are meaningful to himself, and to others.

Fourth, a person needs to feel that he can satisfy his organic or physical functions; that is, that he can gain satisfaction through the important oral, excretory, genital, and motor functions of his body.

Fifth, a person needs to feel that he has a unifying philosophy of life which gives coherence and direction to his existence. By some people this is called man's religious need.

The odds are against finding a mentally healthy person who does not come out pretty well when compared with the above five criteria.

But these five criteria are largely descriptive rather than explanatory in any deep sense. The next question is this: How did the healthy person get to be that way? How did he finally come to possess these five healthy characteristics? Here again, the causes, the developmental determinants, are quite well known and understood. Very simply, it took the mature love of understanding parents (or their substitutes) to accomplish the development of a mature child who later became a mature adult. The mental health of a person did not just happen. It was caused, and it was caused by important people in the child's nearby world who could transmit the love and support and concern and understanding and acceptance and emotional generosity which "caught on" in the child.

The five characteristics are all learned—every one of them. None of us was born with a single one of them. They can be—in fact, must be—learned early in life. The odds are against learning them very well after the age of 16 or 18. Psychoanalytic psychotherapy, which makes the most thorough attempt, cannot do in five years of thrice-weekly treatment what a mature and loving mother could have done more effectively in a much, much shorter time at a much earlier age. Lacking a loving early environment, a person is forever after handicapped to some extent. Of course, there can be repairing experiences which can go a long way in offsetting familial damage. Perceptive and accepting teachers, ministers, relatives, older friends, etc., can do much of what a parent left undone. But unless such repairing experiences come at a fairly early age, it will always be extremely difficult for that deprived person to receive and to give love and to take responsibility—which are the identifying marks of a healthy person.

DOES FAITH AFFECT EMOTIONAL HEALTH?

Now it is time to ask the question again: But how does one's Christian faith affect the person? Recalling again the five essentials of good emotional integration noted above, we can say that none of the five is unique to any one religious faith. They can exist in a person quite apart from any formal creed. This may be a hard saying for many Christians (particularly of a conservative turn of mind) to accept. Yet, specialists in the field of mental health would be virtually unanimous in their belief that it is loving relationships with people, particularly early in life, which produce good mental health. These relationships build into the child the personality strength necessary to withstand the normal stresses of life, or even greater than normal stresses. Every person who lives has an emotional breaking point, of course, but that breaking point will come much later to a person who has been reared in such a way that he learned that he is a decent person, capable of having good times with most people, and able to enjoy the normal functions of his own body, and all of this being done in some kind of wider (at least worldwide, or cosmic) context in which he feels at home.

Does, then, a Christian believer, because he is a believer, have unique resources which enable him to become and to remain more emotionally mature? The answer to such a question must be both yes and no.

There are unquestionably such resources within the Christian faith, and particularly within the church, i.e., the fellowship or community of believers. These resources do much to enable believers to be better integrated emotionally. The powerful beliefs of the Christian, if carried out in observable behavior with one's neighbor, can be powerful deeds for the betterment of the neighbor's mental health.

But there must be this caution. If the great Christian ethic truly takes hold within the Christian community, the results may *include* better mental health. There can be, however, a vast gulf between what ought to happen and what actually does happen in the average Christian congregation. In actual practice, very little might happen which promotes emotional wholeness, despite the noble teachings of Jesus. If these teachings do not become immeshed in a person's behavior, then, of course, they are of no value to himself or to his neighbor. This may be the prevailing situation in the lives of many professed followers of Jesus.

Does the Christian, because he is a Christian, gain emotional resources? In answering the question, let us make a rather arbitrary distinction between the act of believing per se as contrasted with the living of one's life within the Christian community, the fellowship of the concerned.

Let us use a hypothetical example of a solitary wanderer, a Robinson Crusoe of the desert. This solitary man chances upon a New Testament, reads it for the first time in his life, and says, "Yes, I believe in Jesus Christ." He makes his assent and becomes a Christian. The question again now: While remaining in his solitariness, apart from any other believer, will his mental health improve? That is, will his ability to receive and to give love and to take responsibility increase? The answer is that his mental health will probably not improve very much. Emotional health generally does not improve in isolation from other persons. One generally cannot sit in a corner alone and meditate and gain much mental health. Such changes usually occur only in relationships with other people. Of course there are exceptions. But we must concern ourselves here with the optimum way and not with possible exceptions. And the optimum way of improving mental health is through close communication with mature people.

In order to know what might happen to the solitary desert wanderer when he becomes a Christian believer, we would have to know the circumstances of his conversion. What led to it? Why was he receptive? With what conflicts did he wrestle? Some persons might appear to be better integrated, and others not, after such an experience.

The experience that *could* certainly begin to improve his mental health would be for him to get into contact with other Christians in a fellowship marked by love and concern. It would be the acceptance of himself by this group that could bring about some definite changes in his personality.

The distinction that is being made here is between the act of belief itself and the living of one's life in the midst of a truly Christian fellowship. The act of belief as such accomplishes little in the way of permanent emotional change. It is within the life of the church that emotional benefits may result—and then only if in the church there are mature Christians who foster among themselves an increasing sense of community, while at the same time actively promoting each individual's progressive realization of his own unique capacities. This is what brings mental health.

Thus, there are two answers to the question of whether or not being a Christian brings benefits in mental health. The act of belief itself accomplishes few, if any, such permanent results. But it is in the living of a Christian life in a devotedly Christian community that the atmosphere for such growth can be provided.

And yet, even with all the good results of living in a Christian community, we should not expect too much. The forces in one which make for emotional difficulty may often be even stronger than the healing forces of a Christian community. Let us review here some of the symptoms of emotional troubles: In the case of a neurotic person, for example, there is usually the feeling that he has not been loved, is not loved, or even cannot be loved. Such people feel guilty and inferior and inadequate without reason. They have a constant sense of dread and fear. They may suffer from chronic tiredness, nervous tension, excessive shyness, sleeplessness, overconscientiousness, a more or less constant fear of physical illness, inability to get along with people, or they may have to prove constantly how good or smart or important they are.

The beginnings of these feelings can be traced back to very early childhood. These feelings are not under the conscious control of the adult who feels that way. A person is not entirely master of himself; he is generally not always in his own complete control. The reason for this is that the broad foundation of one's personality is much larger than just consciousness, i.e., what one can think about. The conscious part is only the superstructure. The whole human inheritance, plus all one's learning, and the experiences of even the first days of life—all this together comprises the unconscious mind. Behavior, and also desires and feelings, are all determined or modified by the unconscious part of a person. The result is that one is not even aware of many of the true motives which shape his course of action. Thus it is usually true that one can no more cure himself of a serious emotional disturbance than he could perform a surgical operation on himself.

It is for this reason that Christians must be most modest in their claims that their faith brings about emotional integration. Personality is formed in accordance with some pretty well understood principles. The process of healing a poorly integrated personality is also quite well understood. The early damage to a personality may be so great that the healing must be so intense that it may be accomplished only in a psychotherapy consultation room, and perhaps not even there. Neurotic problems may be so intense that they are unmovable by such things as will power, determination, intestinal fortitude, etc. It is asking the wrong thing of the Christian faith that it should be able to heal such disorders. The Chrstian faith is not meant to be used as a therapeutic method. While some of the important side effects of Christian faith and life *may* include better emotional integration, experience with Christian people has definitely proved that this is not invariably true. To say to a neurotic sufferer, "Well, if you would only have more faith . . ." is not only useless, but even damaging. If any volitional act, or any other performance under his conscious control, could relieve his distress, he would have done it.

CONCLUSION

Christianity is not, and cannot be, a therapeutic tool or method. It would be a prostitution of the Gospel to make its purpose the promotion of mental health. Life is more than just mental health, and the Christian message cannot be confined to only one segment of life.

Our respect for the teaching of Christ must at times be based on the fact, not that it makes us feel good, but rather that it upsets us every time we think about it. Jesus himself was unable to alleviate fear in all men, or even in all his closest disciples. Nor was he able to help them always to utilize their fears constructively.

Christianity claims to give man the *answers* to the ultimate questions of life—namely, the questions of his origin, his duty, and his destiny. Psychotherapy, on the other hand, involves a certain therapeutic *method* of uncovering and settling emotional conflicts. There will always be, of course, some inevitable overlap. But the therapist should realize that his essential task is not to give direction to lives. It is only to free a person of unconscious problems so that he is freer to choose the direction in life that he wants to go. The preacher's task is so to illuminate Christ that he will indeed prove to be the way and the truth and the life for every listener.

Preachers, then, should be very cautious about what they promise in terms of emotional gain. If emotional growth should occur as a by-product, then there should be gratefulness for that emotional growth. However, it cannot be promised. At any rate, it does no good to preach about it, since *if* it is going to occur, it will occur only as a by-product of preaching about the central message of Christianity. The essential task of the preacher is to illuminate Jesus Christ. Out of this illumination should invariably also come a profound consideration of the questions of truth, and value, and morals; of divine will and its application to all social conditions and to all sorts and conditions of men.

What should the church do then? The church should promote good mental health as a matter of course, along with a hundred other worthy causes. The church should promote it, but be careful to add that its traditional resources—the Word, the Sacraments, and the communion of saints—are not apt to do the job well in many, many instances. Mental health will only be an occasional by-product to the more essential tasks of the church.

The church is going to be in a much more consistent position when it no longer claims that mental health is one of its special provinces. It will relieve the guilt of a lot of pastors when the day comes that it is acceptable to admit frankly that Christians do not necessarily have better dispositions, or sweeter smiles, or healthier personalities—nor should they be expected to have them as a result of their faith. Such a viewpoint might also reassure nonmembers that the church is not filled with hypocrites, since believers will not pretend that they should invariably be more emotionally mature as a result of their presence within the Christian church.

It is a blight on the church that it has too easily claimed that the Christian faith typically confers relief from unsuccessful habits, discouraging moods, or unwanted thoughts. Christian experience has sometimes done all this, but more often it has not. In the latter case, Christianity itself has suffered, and perceptive people have rightly blamed the preacher who made such claims.

All other things being equal, it may be accurate to state that the Christian has mental health resources not available to the nonbeliever. The resources of one's faith and the emotional support which comes from being surrounded by fellow believers can be powerful forces in the maintenance of good emotional integration.

Nevertheless, the very strongest factors which virtually determine one's mental health are the family and personal relationships during one's earliest and most formative years. Those influences far outweigh in significance any influences after the teen years. It is for this reason that the integrating influence of even a strong adult faith may be far outweighed by early personal experiences that leave the child with a residue of emotional damage.

Let us, then, remind ourselves that the essential task of the church is to draw men to Christ and into the fellowship of others who also follow him and his teachings. If one *feels* better for it, let him be most modest in his claims, because his neighbor who believes equally well may *not* feel better.

Let us take mental health off the list of Christian virtues and put it where it rightly belongs—as a quality of life resulting primarily from early, close associations with mature people. That Christians should seek this quality of life is certain. It is unwarranted to expect that one's faith in any way should guarantee this quality of life known as good mental health.

VIII

The Secular: Threat or Mandate?

LOREN E. HALVORSON

The term "secularism" is becoming increasingly difficult to define. In the nineteenth century the word "secularism" denoted an intellectual revolt against theological domination in the sciences. In Roman Catholic countries it came to refer to the movements seeking independence from ecclesiastical control. Secularism has frequently been defined as practical atheism. The difficulty in definition lies in the fact that secularism denotes no single clearly defined concept, but rather a stance toward God and the world revealed most distinctly in its practical consequences. For many in our day God has simply gone unnoticed because so much of our attention has been riveted with a mixture of fascination and fear on spectacular scientific achievements and global events. "Today we interpret secularism [Latin: *saeculum*—age, or temporal or earthly life] in a very general way as a world and philosophy of life set free from the Christian faith and originating out of a spirit of innerworldliness."[1]

The term "secular" has thus become suspect in the church, and in preventing any further encroachment of

[1] Hans Heinrich Wolf, "Säkularismus," *Evangelische Soziallexikon* (Stuttgart: Kreuz-Verlag, 1954), p. 878. (Translation mine in all quotes unless otherwise indicated.)

DR. HALVORSON is assistant director, Board of College Education, The American Lutheran Church, Minneapolis, Minn.

secularism in our churches we are prone to avoid the "secular." This reticence about the profane (literally, that which stands before the temple—*pro-fanum*) is, paradoxically, a factor contributing to the problem of increasing the secularism of the world. Our argument is basically this: The new life in Christ not only frees the believer from a negative view of the secular but also demands his positive participation in the secular. There is no doubt a fear throughout the churches in our urban, industrial, and affluent age that the "world is too much with us." However, the solution is not simply flight from the world, not new forms of monasticism, but a new relationship to the world. As Christians we often fail to take the world seriously in our dismissal of it as "the order of things opposed to God." But the new life in Christ, inaugurated by a denial of the flesh and an abandoning of the world, culminates, nevertheless, in a new, vigorous participation in the world that takes it dead seriously. Secularism is a threat but "secularity" is a clear mandate for the believer.

THE PURSUIT OF THE SECULAR

The beginnings of secularism in the modern age have frequently been traced back to the destruction of the *corpus christianum.*[2] Max Weber saw it as the result of the rationalization of the genius of the religious movements, a process he called the "routinization of *charisma.*"[3] (Charisma in the New Testament Greek refers to the gifts of the Holy Spirit.) When man gained control over his physical environment through the discovery and control of natural laws, his world became "disenchanted."

> The fate of our times is characterized by rationalization and intellectualization and, above all, by the "disenchantment of the world." Precisely the ultimate and most sub-

---

2Cf. for example, Kurt Dietrich Schmidt, *Grundriss der Kirchengeschichte* IV (Göttingen: Vandenhoeck & Ruprecht, 1954), pp. 405 ff.
3Cf. Max Weber, *From Max Weber*, Ed. and trans. by H. H. Girth and C. Wright Mills (London: Routledge and Kegan Paul, Ltd., 1948), pp. 51-55.

lime values have retreated from public life either into the transcendental realm of mystic life or into the brotherliness of direct and personal human relations. It is not accidental that today only within the smallest and intimate circles, in personal human situations, in *pianissimo,* that something is pulsating that corresponds to the prophetic *pneuma,* which in former times swept through the great communities like a firebrand, welding them together.[4]

Weber saw this conflict particularly in intellectual life where the rise of scientific method raised claims conflicting with those of religion.

The tension between religion and intellectual knowledge definitely comes to the fore wherever rational, empirical knowledge has consistently worked through to the disenchantment of the world and its transformation into a causal mechanism. . . . In principle, the empirical as well as the mathematically oriented view of the world develops refutations of every intellectual approach which in any way asks for a "meaning" or inner-worldly occurrences. Every increase of rationalism in empirical science increasingly pushes religion from the rational into the irrational realm; but only today does religion become *the* irrational or anti-rational supra-human power.[5]

The more religion attempts to rationalize the meaning of the world, the greater wedge it drives between the world and that which it considers to be sacred. Weber argued that this only tends toward a greater disenchantment of the world.

Viewed from a purely ethical point of view, the world has to appear fragmentary and devalued in all those instances when judged in the light of the religious postulates of a divine "meaning" of existence. This devaluation results from the conflict between the rational claim and reality, between the ethic and the partly rational, and partly irrational values. With every construction of the specific nature of each special sphere existing in the world, this

4*Ibid.,* p. 155.
5*Ibid.,* pp. 350-351.

conflict has seemed to come to the fore ever more sharply and more insolubly. The need for "salvation" responds to this devaluation by becoming more other-worldly, more alienated from all structural forms of life, and, in exact parallel, by confining itself to the specific religious essence.[6]

Dietrich Bonhoeffer has described the process of secularization in modern times as "the world coming of age." No longer is the world dependent on God. Man has emancipated himself from God. Man has declared himself and his world autonomous.

Man has learned to cope with all questions of importance without recourse to God as a working hypothesis. In questions concerning science, art, and even ethics, this has become an understood thing which one scarcely dares to tilt at anymore. But for the last hundred years or so it has become increasingly true of religious questions also. It is becoming evident that everything gets along without "God," and just as well as before. As in the scientific field, so in human affairs generally, what we call "God" is being more and more edged out of life, losing more and more ground.[7]

God is no longer consulted. Life is organized as if he did not exist. The world has become solely responsible for itself. Natural science and autonomous reason have either been equated with or replaced God. Bonhoeffer illustrates the "age of maturity" in man's faith in unhindered progress, an optimistic culture, claims for the validity of human rights, the social and political revolution of the masses, and materialism. Part of this secularist concern has been to restore man to his rightful position again. But, ironically, the very attempt has deprived man of all that is valuable to him. Apart from God man cannot achieve or regain his status as man. According to LeRoy Loemker the results of secularism are: (1) the impoverishing of the hu-

---

6*Ibid.*, p. 357.
7Dietrich Bonhoeffer, *Prisoner for God*, Trans. by Reginald H. Fuller (New York: Macmillan, 1954), pp. 145-146.

man spirit when it orbits around itself rather than God
and settles in mediocrity, (2) "an aimless pluralism and
confusion in values which dissolves man and society," and
(3) the reduction of man's high religion to cults of super-
stition.

> Creativity withers and our culture is debased to a wor-
> ship of what Toynbee has called "ephemeral selves,
> ephemeral institutions, and ephemeral techniques." The
> very human power to build, to love, and to enjoy is lost
> when it seeks to stand alone, without the life-giving
> powers of God.[8]

The pursuit of the secular as an end in itself, as apart
from a prior loyalty to Christ, has led to destructive results
in emptying man's existence of meaning. The rebellion of
the beatniks and the anguish of many existentialists are
evidences of the hollowness of a secularized culture. It is
precisely because we have viewed our life in the world as
that which stands alone, apart from our life in Christ, that
it has become demonic.

According to Hendrik Van Oyen, man has wrested himself free from God's history and sought to create a parallel
history. He argues that in this profane history man's highest ambitions are frustrated. Man appears to be his own
lord, but in reality he is his own slave.

> Adam becomes subservient to *adama* (Gen. 3:19. Hebrew
> for the ground, out of which Adam was taken). The
> victories of this history are the victories of war rather
> than of peace. The goal of all things is no longer life, but
> death. Existence for man has become an "existence—
> unto death."[9]

Bonhoeffer finds in the French Revolution the roots of
modern secularism. Nationalism, technology, and mass
movements, he argues, can be traced to this great political
and social upheaval. These three forces, in various con-

8Leroy E. Loemker, *The Christian Faith and Secularism*, Ed. by J. Richard Spann
(New York: Abingdon-Cokesbury, 1948), pp. 15-18.
9Hendrik van Oyen, *Evangelische Ethik* I (Basel: F. Reinhardt, 1952), p. 45.

figurations, opposed each other and resulted in disharmony.

> The masses and nationalism are hostile to reason. Technology and the masses are hostile to nationalism. Nationalism and technology are hostile to the masses.[10]

Technology has led to the enslavement of man by the machine. Nationalism has led to war. The emancipation of the masses has made deadly foes of men. The process of secularism has robbed the Western world of its unity and brought it to the brink of the void. "Everything established is threatened with annihilation. This is not a crisis among other crises. It is a decisive struggle of the last days."[11]

Bonhoeffer describes the demonic aspect of this ultimate range of secularism.

> As an apostasy from all that is established it is the supreme manifestation of all the powers which are opposed to God. It is the void made god. No one knows its goal or its measure. Its dominion is absolute. It is a creative void, which blows its anti-god's breath into the nostrils of all that is established and awakens it to a false semblance of new life while sucking out from it its proper essence, until at last it falls in ruin as a lifeless husk and is cast away. The void engulfs life, history, family, vocation, language, faith. The list can be prolonged indefinitely, for the void spares nothing.[12]

A POST-CHRISTIAN PHENOMENON

Secularism as practical atheism has been known in every age. Men like Machiavelli, Hobbes, Paine, Comte, Holyoake and movements such as Marxism, Darwinism, and many political "isms," suggest variations on this theme. What is unique, however, about secularism today

---

10Dietrich Bonhoeffer, *Ethics*, Trans. by Neville Horton Smith (London: SCM Press, 1955), p. 38.
11*Ibid.*, p. 41.
12*Ibid.*, p. 42.

is, first, its pervasiveness, and, secondly, its post-Christian character. It has become so much a part of our existence that we are frequently not even aware of it. Most Americans, no doubt, were indignant at the Russian criticism of the American exhibit in Moscow (1959) as being "materialistic." Thirdly, secularism in the West must be understood as a post-Christian phenomenon. In Bonhoeffer's phrase, the world has "come of age." "The Christian gospel receives its most devasting blows, often unconsciously, from those who stand within a long Christian inheritance but who now pass it by in preoccupation with much that seems more exciting."[13] In the words of Oldham, we are witnesses of the "emergence of a consciously post-Christian world" through the "progressive paganism" of thought and life.[14] "The world has known Christ and has turned its back on Him."[15] Only a world which was once Christian can be as godless as our modern world. Only a world that has ceased to be an object of religious worship (as in the Christian view of the world) could become as removed from the realm of faith as is the modern world.

The man of this post-Christian world has been skillfully described by Jan Christian Hoekendijk as the "fourth man."[16] This man, says Hoekendijk, is incapable of revolution or revival. He is able to reflect only on what his age no longer is. He is not anti-something, but post-something. He is post-bourgeois. He has lost his certainties, even his fales ones. He is post-Christian. The church cannot reawaken the faith of his youth but must rather do real missionary work in which nothing can be assumed. He is post-churchly. The church as an institution has simply lost all meaning for him. This "fourth man" is also post-personal. The "I" is no longer the center of the subject, but an object

---

13Georgia Harkness, *The Modern Rival to Christian Faith* (New York: Abingdon-Cokesbury, 1952), p. 11.
14J. H. Oldham, *The Resurrection of Christendom* (London: The Sheldon Press, 1940), p. 21.
15Bonhoeffer, *Ethics*, p. 44.
16Jan Christian Hoekendijk, "Ende und Anfang der Verkündigung," *Quatember* XVII (Easter, 1953), 70-75. Cf. also his article, "Die Theologie des Vierten Menschen," *Die Neue Furche* VII (June, 1953), 391-397.

which is threatened from all sides and which seeks security and obscurity in the mass.

THE CHRISTIAN ROOTS OF SECULARITY

That religion, and specifically Christianity, is in some way involved in the rise of secularism has been argued by several scholars. Rudolf Sohm, the German church historian, traced the roots of secularism to the shift from charismatic to bureaucratic authority in the early church. He maintained that in place of the irrational, divine authority of charisma (i.e., the gift of the Holy Spirit) there emerged a rational, systematic formula of one's duty as it was logically deduced from the Christian message. The preaching of the church was rationalized into dogmas, charisma into a legal order, and faith into a matter of submission to certain doctrines. Divine authority passed from the individual to the congregation and finally to the hierarchical church government based on a legal-traditional type of authority. Charisma ultimately became the sole property of the church councils. Sohm traced this transformation of authority from a divinely led assembly of believers to a rigid institution guided by purely human orders.[17] What Max Weber described as the disenchantment of the world, Sohm had spoken of earlier as the transformation of charisma into the everyday (*Alltag*). He saw this occurring particularly in the secularization of the Holy Spirit into church doctrines and legal codes.

Beginning at another point in church history, Ernst Troeltsch has also developed the thesis that out of the Christian church has come a strong impulse toward the secularization of the world. In an essay entitled "Luther, Protestantism and the Modern World," Troeltsch developed the general theme that Luther's thought marks a break with the sacramental view of the world and places

---

[17]Cf. Rudolf Sohm, *Kirchenrecht*, I (Leipzig: Verlag von Duncker und Humboldt, 1892), pp. 160 f., 216, 227, 458. A similar argument is found in his *Wesen und Ursprung des Katholizismus* (Leipzig: Verlag von B. G. Teubner, 1912), pp. 51-56.

the main emphasis on the basic conviction that religion is faith.[18] Luther transferred religion out of the sphere of sacramental miracle and into the sphere of thought and spirit. The first principle resulting from this significant shift was that religion itself was psychologized and its mystery sank completely into the hidden depths of the affairs of the soul. The second principle that Troeltsch saw in Luther's thought was the emphasis on religious individualism as opposed to ecclesiastical and authoritative religion. The third principle was the understanding of the religious idea as something coherent and rational.

> It [religion] is not an incomprehensible miracle-working sacrament whose spiritual results can be accomplished only through laborious preparation and obscure magic. It is rather an idea out of whose innermost character the religious and ethical effects are logically and psychologically deduced and understood.[19]

The fourth principle which Troeltsch noted resulted from Luther's removal of the antithesis between the worldly life and the monastic ideal of flight from the world. The Reformer laid the theological basis for wholehearted participation in the natural circumstances of life and in historically conditioned civilization.

> Miracle is defined not simply as supernatural or as the power of divine magic over nature, but it is seen as the restoring of man to his own true essence, the true ground of being, authenticated and made apprehensible for us in Christ through the revelation of merciful love. The sphere of the miraculous activity is thus no longer that of supernature with its corresponding supernatural performances, but rather the simple fulfilling of the sphere of natural activities with the pure and simple miracle of the inner disposition of trust in and union with God. To this extent Goethe was right in extolling Luther as "the man who has once more had the courage to stand firmly on God-given earth."[20]

18Ernst Troeltsch, *Gesammelte Schriften* IV (Tübingen: J. C. B. Mohr, 1925), pp. 216-230.
19*Ibid.*, p. 221.
20*Ibid.*, pp. 223-224.

Troeltsch maintained that under the influence of modern life these four principles (viz., faith alone, religious individualism, religion as inwardness or idea, and secular vocation) led to the basic tenets of "modern Protestantism." Though modern Protestantism departs fundamentally at several points from Luther's solid biblical orientation, nevertheless its initial foundation was laid by him. The radical changes were finally realized through the decline of ecclesiastical domination, the renewed sanctioning of national political and economic life in the modern state, the influx of revived Renaissance culture, and the scientific thrust of the Enlightenment. The results of this change were a purely secular state, a rational and mercantile economy, and an unrestricted critical science and art. Troeltsch concluded with these words:

> There is a continuity between them [the "old" and the "new" Protestantism] in so far as the Protestant countries from the outset presented much less opposition to the establishment of this modern culture and offered a point of contact with their qualified (even more than justified by conscience) acceptance of secular life. This acceptance took place slowly, bit by bit, without the new consequences being immediately apparent. It took place under the official claim that this was only the further development of Protestantism's accepted elements of natural morality, natural revelation of God, and the natural unfolding of the consequences of redeemed secular, political and economic life. . . . The imperceptibility of the transition is in point of fact proof that there is an inner continuity between "inner-worldly asceticism" and the complete acceptance of the secular world. . . . Modern religious thought and life must be seen in this way to be the consequences of the main thrust of the Reformation.[21]

SECULARISM OR SECULARIZATION?

Another German theologian a generation after Troeltsch has also traced the rise of modern secularism to the Christian

---

[21]*Ibid.,* pp. 229-230.

faith. Friedrich Gogarten has developed the thesis that we can best understand secularism when we consider it as an integral part of the Christian faith. First, we must understand its roots in the Christian faith before we can properly understand the nature of modern secularism and its defection from its ancestral home. Gogarten argued that by the term "secularization" we ought not to mean the process by which Christianity loses its other-worldly character and dissolves its dynamic in the world, but, rather, we should define this process in terms of Christianity's initial concern to make the world nothing more than just the world, i.e., the *created* order. The Christian faith frees men from false religious views of the world. It "de-mythologizes" the world. The Christian faith declares the world to be world and nothing more. This is what we ought to mean by the "secularization" of the world.

> The first and most important thing which is to be said about the relation of the Christian faith to the world is the complete freedom of man from the world. This freedom belongs to the essence of the Christian faith. Without it it is not possible for it to be the faith and profession of God which it is. Through this freedom it distinguishes itself from all ante-Christian forms of religious piety, from the heathen as well as the Jewish. . . . It is the ordered, law-bound world, from which the Christian faith makes one free.[22]

The Apostle Paul speaks of our freedom from the law as freedom from the στοιχεῖα, i.e., freedom from the powers of this world to which man so naturally and willingly gives his allegiance rather than to God. When man worships the creature rather than the Creator, he sins. However, where Gnostic theories would conclude from this that the Christian should separate himself from the "evil" world, the Christian view argues for man's responsibility for the world as God's creation. The antithesis to God is not the world as such, but the world as the "fallen" or "corrupt"

22Friedrich Gogarten, *Verhängnis und Hoffnung der Neuzeit* (Stuttgart: Friedrich Vorwerk Verlag, 1953), pp. 12-13.

order which actively opposes God. Gogarten's concern is
that the church, in the battle against secularism, not lose the
healthy biblical understanding of the world as God's
creation. If we understand "world" as the realm of the
demonic, then for the Christian there is an end of the
world and the coming of the new age. But "world" can
also mean simply the orders of state, family, society, i.e.,
the orders of creation. We cannot be completely hostile to
it since it is the realm in which Christ lived. In order to
distinguish between these two views of the world, Gogarten uses two terms: "secularization" as the positive
acceptance of the created order, and "secularism" as the
process by which the world as an autonomous realm independent of God becomes demonic. Despite the form which
the process of secularization has taken in modern times,
Gogarten insists it is a legitimate result of the Christian
faith.[23]

Gogarten is not alone in attempting to find another term
to preserve the positive thrust toward the world. Heinz-
Dietrich Wendland uses the term "legitimate profanity"
to describe the process of secularization accomplished
when Christ defeated the demonic cosmic powers.[24] But
this profanity, warns Wendland, exists only where Christ
is acknowledged as the Παντοκράτωρ (the Almighty, Rev.
1:8) and the Κύριος (Lord) of the world. "The release from
the world which the Christian message declares is also a
release from the toil, the fruitless labor, the pursuit of
money and property, success and security. This view is inseparable from the eschatological realism of the message
of Christ who is our hope. . . . The 'new' world, the redeemed and restored world is a new creation in the sense
of the beginning of the fulfillment. Therefore it can be
called the 'holy profanity.' "[25]

---

[23]Friedrich Gogarten, *Der Mensch Zwischen Gott und Welt* (Stuttgart: Vorwerk-
Verlag, 1956), pp. 139 ff.
[24]Heinz-Dietrich Wendland, *Die Kirche in der Modernen Gesellschaft* (Hamburg:
Furche Verlag, 1956), p. 51.
[25]*Ibid.*, p. 117.

Secularism, it might then be argued, is not so much a new heathen philosophy as a *Christian heresy*. This point is obscured, however, when the church takes only a belligerent stance toward all that which is associated with secularism. But when we understand that secularism is the peculiar product of a post-Christian age, that it represents a great biblical motif ripped out of context, that it becomes demonic when separated from the life in Christ, then we are in a better position to resurrect and defend a Christian truth while rejecting its distorted and demonic forms.

A NEW VIEW OF THE WORLD

Although it has become popular in modern theology to lash out against secularism from our protected "Mount Sinais," this is not the only posture proper to the Christian faith. As necessary as it is to draw sharp and clear lines between that which is of God and that which is of the "flesh" (i.e., that which is opposed to God), there is also the necessity for counsel from the church to her members, who must somehow realize their Christian responsibility in the world and are searching for some point of contact between the church and the world upon which to do this. Through his prophets God has pronounced loud and terrible noes to the world, but his affirmation of the world in the Gospel is equally stirring. There are indeed moments when the church is called upon to make thundering denunciations against all that threatens to engulf her in this world. But we must also provide a basis for the Christian's responsible life in the world. Among those who have been concerned particularly with this latter task are some who have employed Luther's two-kingdom theory to maintain this dual emphasis. Unfortunately, however, this doctrine more adequately defends the necessary distinction between these two spheres of the Christian's life than it successfully indicates how the Christian might also relate the two. The orders of creation are frequently cited as the basis of the Christian's responsibility within the secular realm, but this position is poised on the brink of justifying one of the tenets of modern secularism, viz., the autonomy of the world (*Eigengesetzlichkeit*). This "brinkmanship" of the Lutheran social ethic has had fearful consequences and has led some to re-examine the Reformer's position in regard to the world.[26]

Goethe's statement that Luther has set man solidly upon earth is correct in that Luther set the Christian free for service in the world on the basis of his doctrines of justification and the priesthood of all believers. The basis of Luther's acceptance of the world is his realization that man is free toward all things, free to the things below *(nach unten)*.[27] The secular orders are not the place for the Christian to earn his status of acceptability to God, but rather become, in Luther's understanding, the place to render service to one's neighbor in response to God's love. The Christian thus eagerly enters the world to serve, not so much out of a sense of duty to the laws of a created order as in response to the God behind the orders who in Christ has declared him forgiven and free. (There is a strange kind of "gay abandonment" that characterizes the believer's life in the world.) Apart from the Word of God it is meaningless to appeal to the orders of creation as the basis for the Christian's secular responsibility.[28] The doctrine of justification by faith, which sets men free for service in the world, must be the beginning point of Luther's social ethic.

From an over-all perspective which the doctrine of the two kingdoms both deduces and assumes, and which the doctrine of justification as the center of Scriptures estab-

26Cf. Gunnár Hillerdal, *Gehorsam gegen Gott und Menschen* (Göttingen: Vandenhoeck & Ruprecht, 1955), pp. 123 ff.
27Martin Luther, *Werke*, XVIII (Leipzig: H. Baehlou, 1908), pp. 638, 753-754.
28George Forell, *Faith Active in Love* (Minneapolis: Augsburg Publishing House, 1959), pp. 127 ff.

lishes (and that means the justification alone by faith which frees from the demand of the law and denies any work righteousness but at the same time calls for acts of love toward the neighbor by the believer), the whole Protestant ethic and also the teaching of the Christian's role in the state must be seen. . . . What is primary is not the order or station, nor a rational grasping of the demands which the individual accepts out of his obedience to the order. Much more must the point of departure for ethics be the doctrine of justification, the doctrine of the calling of men to deeds of faith and love as disciples of Jesus Christ.[29]

Ernst Wolf underscores this point that the Christian's duty in the orders presupposes the experience of justification. Only in faith do we discover the meaning of the law. This faith drives us to the reality in the natural order whose true meaning only the Gospel can uncover.[30] The Gospel thus frees the Christian to undertake his task in the secular orders because through the Gospel he sees them only as secular. The *mythos* of their autonomy, of their independent laws and rules, is removed. The secular is de-mythologized. The true nature of "world" is discovered.

The de-mythologizing of the orders makes the world worldly and therefore healthy. That is the New Testament view of the "secularization" of the world which establishes its true "profanity." This is realized through the victory of Christ over all cosmic deities and demons. In this sense there is a legitimate profanity and a healthy and beneficial secularization.[31]

SECULARITY AND THE NEW LIFE IN CHRIST

The new life in Christ makes it possible for the Christian to assume more than one stance toward the world. While denying the claims of autonomy of modern secularism, he

---

29Hillerdal, *op. cit.*, p. 51.
30Ernst Wolf, "Natürliches Gesetz und Gesetz Christi bei Luther," *Evangelische Theologie*, 1935, pp. 305 ff.
31Wendland, *op. cit.*, p. 51.

still maintains a healthy thrust toward the world as the arena in which God calls him to serve his neighbor. If we understand secularism as a Christian heresy, we can then also recover the truth it obscures. Freed from the world, the Christian is free to accept it and enter it in obedience to Christ's call to discipleship.

We turn now to consider briefly the implications of our argument that the locus of the life in Christ is in the world. "God was in Christ reconciling the world to himself," and the Christian therefore, as an "agent of reconciliation," finds that he has very much to do with the world.[32] The proper index, then, for the believer's "churchmanship" is not the number of hours spent in the structures of the congregation, but rather the quality of his life in the world, and primarily in his occupation. It would follow that the task of the local congregation is not to provide religious activities for the members so that they can thereby discharge their responsibilities for witness and service, but rather to prepare the members for a significant ministry in the world.

This immediately leads to a second implication, namely, the vital role of the laity. The laity, far more than any professional Christian workers, represent the point at which the church makes contact with the world. They are the frontiersmen today who occupy the critical positions for the missionary tasks in "foreign" territories almost completely removed from the church's life and witness. Furthermore, because of the sociological and ecclesiastical isolation of the professional minister, it has become a matter of utmost urgency that the neglected ministry of the laity be recovered. To the degree that the church has failed to equip the laity for the ministry (Eph. 4:12) and to direct them off the church premises and into their own worlds, to that degree the church has contributed to the secularism of our culture. We need not be afraid of speak-

---

32Cf. Arnold Come, *Agents of Reconciliation* (Philadelphia, Westminster, 1960).

ing of the secularity of the life in Christ and of facing up to the consequent revolution that this implies in the present "parish building centered" life of the American church. If the church is to take a fresh and serious look at the role of the laity, this implies also taking the world of the laity seriously. The church must deal with the problems, the pathos, the penultimates of the layman's occupational life with precision and objectivity. Many laymen do not feel their daily life addressed by the pulpit because the pastor is frequently ignorant of the kind of universe in which his parishioners live. The pastor's acquaintance with his people's existence outside the congregational activity may extend to their residential life, but seldom does it go much beyond that. In addition the layman finds little to help him relate ultimate, theological questions to the penultimate issues with which he deals daily. Some way must be found to meet the layman in his world in order to understand it and minister in it. No doubt some pioneer ventures are called for, involving calculated risks and hardships, but this is one of the fronts on which the church must do battle today.[33]

A fourth implication of our thesis is the need for the church to be willing to surrender her prerogatives and become incarnate in the life of her people. Christ has set us free from absolute allegiances to everything save to himself. We can therefore willingly undergo, if necessary, a kind of *kenosis* (Phil. 2:7), an emptying of ourself and of the existing structures of the church in order to identify the presence of the kingdom in the midst of our age. Some clearer demonstration of the humanity of Christ is needed to restore a sense of vocation to our people's daily work. Their "jobs" may become joyful occasions for loving serv-

33Cf., for example, Margaret Frakes, *Bridges to Understanding* (Philadelphia: Muhlenberg, 1960) ; George W. Webber, *God's Colony in Man's World* (New York: Abingdon-Cokesbury, 1960) ; G. Michennaux, *Revolution in a City Parish* (Philadelphia: Westminster, 1956) ; Gibson Winter, *The Suburban Captivity of the Churches* (Garden City: Doubleday, 1961) ; Lydia Praeger, *Frei für Gott und die Menschen* (Stuttgart: Quell-Verlag, 1959).

ice when they realize that God is at work "in, with, and under" the typewriter, machine press, acetylene torch, and artist's brush.

Finally, our thesis concerning the secularity of the life in Christ provides a necessary balance to the growing tendency of the church to go on retreats. There is no question but that the church desperately needs the inner renewal that can come from quiet periods of meditation, of an inner dialogue with God and with fellow believers. It is only *in* Christ that we can recover the dynamic which enables us to colonize the world. But there is a danger that the church may thereby retreat from a genuine encounter and dialogue with the secular. If Christians retire into a small, intimate cell to be closeted with the Lord, then they must be alerted at the same time to the secularity of the life that Christ intends for us. It is significant that even as he prayed that his disciples might be one with him and with each other, he also prayed that they might remain *in* the world (John 17:15). The secular world remains a threat to the church, but the believer is nevertheless under a mandate to live in it with a serious joy.

IX

Architecture and the Protestant Community

OSMUND R. OVERBY

By the sixteenth century Western man no longer saw himself in a Gothic world. First the Renaissance, and then the Reformation, had affected his view of the world and also of himself in that world. These attitudes found expression in a world of new forms with which he surrounded himself, beginning in Italy early in the fifteenth century and spreading thoughout Europe.

In the history of art, the Reformation, in contrast to the Renaissance, has usually been considered only as a cold north wind that caused widespread and terrible destruction. The iconoclasm that followed in its wake—the loss of great treasures of religious paintings, sculpture, and stained glass, and the disfigurement of countless churches —has made such an impression on historians that the question of Protestantism in its early stages having a fructifying influence on art has seldom been raised.[1]

Though most Protestant communities, with a sense of righteousness, dispensed with painting, sculpture, and in some cases even music, they could not get along without buildings to worship in, and wherever the political situation

---

[1]For example, Ernest Short, *A History of Religious Architecture* (3rd rev. ed., London: Eyre & Spottiswoode, 1951), a standard work, only discusses Protestant iconoclasm before considering the Anglican architecture of Inigo Jones and Sir Christopher Wren.

MR. OVERBY is a graduate student, Department of the History of Art, Yale University, New Haven, Conn.

187

allowed, they adapted old churches or built new ones in ways expressive of their new forms of worship. The story of these early Protestant churches has not yet been fully told. It can be seen, however, that these churches have certain common formal characteristics, and that in some ways, at least, they are images of that new world the Protestant reinterpreted for himself.

In a negative way, the effects of Protestantism can be seen on at least two major developments in art history. In southern Europe, the specific pronouncements of the Council of Trent gave rise to a rich Counter-Reformation art that has been carefully studied.[2] And in the north, by freeing artists from religious programs and ecclesiastical commissions, Protestantism certainly contributed in a practical, if negative, way to the development of Dutch landscape and still-life painting in the sixteenth and seventeenth centuries. The implications of this movement, both for the artist's role in society and for the subject matter of painting, have continued to affect art to the present day. While artists were denied official church programs by Protestantism, in their new independence they were free to explore their own religious ideas in art. Seventeenth century Holland could not only foster a still-life painter like Jacob van Ruisdael, but also a Rembrandt, whose painting is in some ways specifically Protestant as well as generally religious.[3]

The early Protestant churches have not only gone unstudied, they have also been largely disguised by later alterations. The death knell of early Protestant church architecture was tolled by the Gothic revival in architecture, which was supported by the various liturgical and ecclesiological revivals of the nineteenth century. Archi-

---

2For a full critical review of the extensive literature on the subject, see C. Galassi Paluzzi, *Storia segreta dello stile dei Gesuiti* (Rome: F. Mondiri, 1951), 105-172.

3This relationship of Protestantism to Dutch painting has been noted by many writers. See, for example, Leslie P. Spelman, "Calvin and the Arts," *Journal of Aesthetics and Art Criticism*, VI (March, 1948), 246-252, who traces it to Calvin; also, S. Slive, "Notes on the Relationship of Protestantism to Seventeenth Century Dutch Painting," *Art Quarterly*, XIX, No. 1 (1956), 2-15.

tecture was espcially affected by the work of the Camden Ecclesiological Society in England, beginning in 1839, and a similar movement in Germany under Karl Wilhelm III before 1840 and Karl Wilhelm IV after.[4] In architectural literature, this new attitude toward church building is marked by the publication in England of Pugin's *Contrasts . . . Showing the Present Decay of Taste* in 1836. Decrying post-Reformation architecture, Pugin argued that medieval styles provided the only suitable catholic architecture. This view prevailed so strongly that later writers on Protestant architecture continued the argument for over a century that Gothic is the suitable style for Protestant churches.[5]

The movement had great success: The plain churches of the early Protestants were remodeled, especially the interiors; various medieval styles were used for new churches; and the medieval churches that had been "purified" for Protestant use in the sixteenth century were "restored." To a large extent, present knowledge of medieval architecture had been conditioned by this revival, which was strong enough, not only to cause the restoration of Gothic churches throughout Europe, but even to bring about the completion of such projects as the great towers on the cathedrals in Cologne and Ulm. The revival affected the Catholic countries also, where Gothic had been as dead as in Protestant areas. In France the cathedrals were sometimes nearly rebuilt under such notable architects as Viollet-le-Duc.

The question of the influence of the Reformation on art is very complex. Various Protestant communities not only took different attitudes toward art, but the art of the sixteenth and seventeenth centuries was also affected by sec-

---

4Several architects participated actively in the work of the Camden Ecclesiological Society; its influence was spread through the publication of *The Ecclesiologist*, of which 189 numbers appeared between November, 1841, and December, 1868. Indicative of this movement in America was the rising social acceptance of the Episcopal Church; even Benjamin Franklin, in spite of his Puritan ancestors and his Puritan ideals, took a pew in Christ Church in Philadelphia and is buried in its cemetery.

5See, for example, George Gordon Coulton, *Art and the Reformation* (New York: Alfred A. Knopf, 1928).

ular forces, ranging from local traditions to the humanism of the Renaissance. To identify the Protestant aesthetic would be as impossible as describing the Protestant philosophy. Only within carefully defined limits could one begin looking for Protestant artistic styles.

This study will survey the question of the influence of the Reformation on the church architecture of various early Protestant communities. It can be seen that this architecture is, in certain general ways, distinctly Protestant in that it was affected by Protestant ideas and worship requirements. It can also be seen that this architecture developed in different ways under varying Protestant attitudes toward art, and that in some instances it became a unified artistic expression of certain forms of Protestantism.

LUTHER AND CALVIN ON PROTESTANT CHURCHES

From the beginning, both conservative and liberal tendencies in artistic and architectural matters developed among the Protestants. The conservative attitude can be seen in Luther's writings, and the more liberal attitude in Calvin's.

The work of the painter and engraver Lucas Cranach is illustrative of the Lutheran impact on the arts generally. One of Luther's friends over a long period of time, Cranach has been called the most faithful artistic exponent of Lutheran Protestantism.[6] Though he was a devoted follower of Luther, Cranach continued to paint pictures of mythological subjects, and it is rather in his portraiture, where the pictorial and decorative elements decreased and Cranach concentrated more and more on the image of the human character, that we can see the influence of his religious views.

For Luther the treatment or the decoration of the churches was not a question of central importance. Though he was

6Otto Benesch, *The Art of the Renaissance in Northern Europe* (Cambridge, Mass.: Harvard University Press, 1945), p. 58. On the close relationship between Cranach and Luther, see pp. 59-61.

repeatedly called on for guidance in the matter of removing images from the churches, he maintained that this and related activities were nonessential aspects of religion. He saw as much spiritual danger in the prevalent iconoclasm as in the presence of images themselves within the churches. In 1525 in "Against the Heavenly Prophets in the Matter of Images and Sacraments,"[7] Luther's reply to Karlstadt and his followers, the Heavenly Prophets, Luther argued that images must be destroyed in the heart, then they become innocuous outside the heart, as indeed they seem to have been for Luther himself. He feared that a disorderly, rowdy destruction of the existing images in the churches would be taken as a good work of the spirit, engendering pride. Luther considered the image-breaking and the destruction of the old churches, as well as the manhandling of the Sacraments by the Heavenly Prophets, a new kind of mortification, a self-chosen putting to death of the flesh. In their practices— no images, no churches, substitution in the Sacraments, a gray peasant garb—he saw a new monkery and a threat to the primacy of the Word of God.

Luther argued that if religious images are spiritually dangerous, the battle against them can be fought only in the Christian's heart, and once the battle has been won there, the images do, indeed, become innocuous. In March, 1522, in his "Eight Sermons at Wittenberg," following the disturbances there the previous December and January led by Karlstadt, Zwilling, and the Zwickau prophets, Luther carefully distinguished between essentials and nonessentials.[8] He said, "When the common man learns that it is not a service to God to place images in the

---

7 *Luther's Works*, XL, ed. Conrad Bergendoff (Philadelphia: Muhlenberg Press, 1958), 73-223.

8 *Luther's Works*, XXXVI, ed. Abdel Ross Wentz (Philadelphia: Muhlenberg Press, 1959), 239 ff. These disturbances in Wittenberg started on December 3, 1521, led by students, and broke out again on Christmas Eve, affecting the parish and castle churches. On Christmas Day, Karlstadt preached against organs, images, and Gregorian chanting, and led an "evangelical" mass in which both kinds of the Sacrament were administered while in street garb. Popular feeling was further aroused when on January 11 Zwilling and a band of monks destroyed altars and cast out images from the churches. Finally the city council set January 24 as the day for the orderly removal of images from the parish church, but the populace could not wait, and did it themselves.

churches, he will cease doing it of his own accord without your assistance. He will have pictures painted on the walls only because he likes them or for decoration or some other reason that does not involve sin. How did we ever get into this predicament, that man should forbid us to do what God has not forbidden, particularly they who are struggling against human teachings and ordinances?"[9]

Luther parted company with the iconoclasts so far as to suggest the use of images and pictures in the church. He made the point that it is the worship of images, not the making of them, that is sinful. The narratives of the Bible inevitably engender mental images, Luther argued, and since I have a "mental image . . . in my heart . . . why should it be a sin to have it in my eyes?"[10] Luther went so far as to suggest a program in which Bible stories would be illustrated not only in books, but also on the walls, inside and out, of the churches.

Luther neither called for a radical program of changing the old churches, nor did he envision a new form of church architecture. In this, as in other practical social matters which he saw as nonessentials of faith, Luther took a conservative and traditionalistic position. In contrast, Calvin took a more severe, specific, and practical position in regard to the arts, and developed the position to some lengths.[11]

Calvin distinguished a hierarchy of art on three levels. The highest art is that of God's system and creation. The next level is the art in the beauty of nature as it shows God's creative power. The lowest level, which is sinful and inspired by the devil, is that art designed purely for man's enjoyment. Calvin traces the origin of this false art, which either exists for its own sake or serves pagan interests outright, to the Greeks.

9*Luther's Works*, XXXVI, 259-260.
10In "Against the Heavenly Prophets in the Matter of Images and Sacraments," *Luther's Works*, XL, 99-100.
11See, principally, Léon Wencelius, *L'Esthétique de Calvin* (Société d'édition "Les Belles Lettres," Paris, 1937) ; also Spelman, *op. cit.*, and Abraham Kuyper, *Calvinism*, Stone Lectures (New York: Revell, 1899).

Calvin admitted both music and poetry in public worship, recognizing their emotional force, although the music could be only simple unison singing, without harmonization and without instrumental support.[12] In contrast to Luther, he prohibited painting and sculpture as ecclesiastical aids to worship, although he did allow them outside the church.

Calvin required two things of ecclesiastical architecture. It must functionally satisfy the needs of the worship ceremony, a practical and comparatively simple problem, and it must be an earthly image of the Spirit leading the faithful in the way of holiness. This second requirement is a perceptive recognition of the power of artistic forms to be expressive in a specific way regardless of literal content or subject matter. With the figural arts excluded from the church, this requirement could not be solved illustratively or metaphorically, but only abstractly through the handling of the forms and the architectural ornament. This radical aesthetic, calling for new forms to express the new truths of Protestantism, distinguishes Calvin's position from Luther's traditionalistic acceptance of the old churches and his paramount concern for order in the removal of images.

Calvin looked to divine activity for a guide in achieving this new architecture, and called for the perfection of the architectural ensemble, for which the human body is the most perfect example.[13] He considered the problem of the ensemble as threefold: the relationship of the parts to the whole, the nuances of part to part, and the harmony of the totality. Architectural decoration must be sober, but it must also have an elegance based on a refined sense of measure, and a splendor which Calvin saw as the beauty in all authentic creative activity.

12In the preface to the edition of his liturgy of 1542, Calvin wrote: "Truly, we know from experience that song has the force and the vigor to move and enflame men's hearts so that they invoke and praise God with a zeal most vehement and ardent."
13Wencelius, *op. cit.*, pp. 154 ff.

Though he pointed out that the material beauty of the churches is not a sufficient end in itself, that, indeed, history taught that churches are not necessary at all, Calvin enunciated general controlling principles by which Protestant church building can be evaluated. And in those communities in which the ways of holiness were made clear for daily life by a practical, thorough, Calvinistic ethics, the churches did become earthly images of the new faith.

ORIGINS OF PROTESTANT ARCHITECTURE

Whenever and wherever political conditions in Europe allowed Protestants a measure of security and freedom of expression, they altered their old churches or built new ones, meeting in different ways and to varying degrees Calvin's two requirements of church architecture. Before the end of the seventeenth century, certain functional and formal characteristics of Protestant church building had evolved.[14]

In the Lutheran churches, of which many examples remain, a new emphasis was placed on the pulpit and on preaching, despite the retention of the altar and the liturgy. The late-Gothic Hallenkirche, built when the Dominicans had emphasized preaching, was ideally suited to Lutheran needs, with a pulpit placed halfway down the nave. Luther's toleration of images resulted in the present richness of statuary and carved ornament in the churches in Germany, and in Scandinavia, where the liturgical tradition was even stronger.

---

[14]The principal sources for Protestant church architecture are: K. E. O. Fritsch, *Der Kirchenbau des Protestantismus von der Reformation bis zur Gegenwart* (Berlin: Toeche, 1893) ; J. Pannier, *L'Église Réformée de Paris sous Henri IV* (Paris: Champion, 1911), *L'Église Réformée de Paris sous Louis XIII, 1610-1621* (Paris: Champion, 1922), *L'Église Réformée de Paris sous Louis XIII, de 1621 à 1629 environ* (Paris: Champion, 1932) ; M. D. Ozinga, *De Protestantsche Kerkenbouw in Nederland* (Amsterdam: H. J. Paris, 1924) ; Andrew Landale Drummond, *The Church Architecture of Protestantism* (Edinburgh: T. & T. Clark, 1934). For a useful summary see: Anthony N. Garvan, "Protestant Plain Style before 1630," *Journal of the Society of Architectural Historians*, IX, No. 3 (October, 1950), 4-13. One of the unanswered questions in the history of Protestant architecture is the influence of Jewish and early Christian architectural forms ; see, for example, Helen Rosenau, "The Synagogue and Protestant Church Architecture," *Journal of the Warburg and Courtauld Institutes*, IV, Nos. 1, 2 (January, 1941), 80-84.

In general, the earliest German churches, like other Protestant churches in Europe, employed a rectangular plan with galleries, though, unlike the others, the German churches often retained the chancel. As elsewhere, the churches are characterized by box pews, low roofs, prominent pulpits, and elaborate organs. To the German churches is owed a debt, not for developing an architectural style, but for trying new plans and interior arrangements. At times they experimented with polygonal, L-shape, or other plan forms,[15] and tried different locations for the pulpit in relation to the congregation and the altar.[16]

Though the German churches found various solutions to the requirements of the new worship service, beyond a sense of confined or limited space within them, expressive of a particular Communal Spirit, they did not develop that earthly image of their faith in abstract form called for by Calvin. The churches seem rather to express the prevailing local cultures, and range freely from the simple rural churches with a peasant domesticity to the high baroque of George Bähr's Frauenkirche at Dresden, built in 1722.[17] As Troeltsch has pointed out, the cultural conservatism of Lutheranism has allowed it to flourish under a variety of social situations: the aggressive military state of Gustavus Adolphus, the Lutheran nobility in the Austrian territories, the pietistic peasant democracy in Denmark and Norway, and American democracy.[18] Lutheran architecture, having satisfied the functional requirements of the worship service, was amenable to a variety of formal expressions reflecting the various prevailing traditions.

In Holland, where the Reformed church became well established both under the old traditions of tolerance in

---

[15]As in the L-shaped church at Freudenstadt built in 1601-1608 by Heinrich Schickhardt, Fritsch, *op. cit.*, p. 46; or in the twelve-sided church at Hanau built in 1622-1654, *ibid.*, pp. 48-49.

[16]In 1590 in the Schlosskirche at Schmalkalden, for example, the pulpit was placed axially over the altar; or at Lauenburg, in 1590, the pulpit was placed in front of the altar.

[17]Drummond, *op. cit.*, pp. 29-31, Pl. III.

[18]Ernst Troeltsch, *The Social Teaching of the Christian Churches*, translated by Olive Wyon, 2 vols. (London: George Allen and Unwin, Ltd., 1931), II, 574-575.

the independent trading cities, and with the establishment of a Protestant Dutch state marked by the declaration of independence from Spain in 1581, Protestant church architecture developed an advanced style by the early seventeenth century. The Dutch were not only very successful at adapting the existing Gothic churches to Protestant needs, but their architects experimented with all the basic types to which later English and some American builders turned.

Gothic churches in Holland, with their "purified" interiors of the sixteenth and seventeenth centuries, are best known to us through the paintings of Saenredam and the other masters of architectural interiors.[19] Typically, the high altar was removed and attention was focused on a prominent pulpit either in the center of the nave or in the chancel. The chancel was often filled with seats, and the eastern end of the apse by a large organ. Most striking was the sense of clear, well-lit space achieved by the removal of all sculpture and ornament but the simplest moldings, and by the substitution of clear for colored glass.

The baroque had no appeal for the Dutch, and they were interested in form rather than in color. In their new churches, Dutch architects experimented with three basic plans: the octagon, a centralized Greek cross, and a simple rectangle. The first new church in Holland was the large brick church at Willemstad, a perfect octagon, built in 1595.[20] Simple and symmetrical on the outside, within it had pews of varying lengths arranged across the whole church, facing the pulpit against one wall.[21]

Both other types of churches, though continuing earlier liturgical traditions, simplified the forms and centralized

---

19See, H. Jantzen, *Das niederländische Architecturbild* (Halle: C. A. Kaemmerer & Co., 1908).
20Ozinga, *op. cit.*, pp. 12-19, Pl. 1-3; Garvan, *op. cit.*, p. 6.
21T. J. Wertenbaker, *The Founding of American Civilization, The Middle Colonies* (New York: Charles Scribner's Sons, 1938), pp. 77-79, has suggested that this church was the source of the eight-sided buildings that were common in and around early New York.

the interiors. The Greek cross plan, with wide, intersecting transepts of short but equal length and a central pulpit placed near the crossing, was widely known in northern Europe. Externally, the Dutch churches were impressive, with soaring roofs and high steeples. Inside, they were well lighted by large windows, rendering the forms clear and distinct. There was no altar, seldom even a communion table, and little symbolism, but finely carved organ cases, pulpits, and magistrates' stalls.

The simple rectangular church, which became the most common Protestant plan in Europe and America, found archetypal expression in a church of great influence designed by the French architect Salomon de Brosse, who is best known as the architect of the Luxembourg Palace in Paris. After Henry IV granted religious freedom to the Protestants through the Edict of Nantes in 1598, the Huguenots built a number of churches throughout France. Most famous of these was the second temple at Charenton near Paris, built 1623-1624, and designed by de Brosse.[22] Charenton, like several other Huguenot churches in France, was a large building seating 5,000.[23] It had a simple rectangular exterior with a huge hip roof, and on the inside there were two tiers of galleries around all four sides. The high pulpit stood free of one end so that the preacher was surrounded by his congregation. This building, with nearly all other Protestant churches in France, was destroyed following the revocation of the Edict of Nantes in 1685.[24] With the end of religious toleration in France, the Huguenots were dispersed throughout Protestant Europe and eventually America, carrying with them their traditions in church building.

---

[22] J. Pannier, *Salomon de Brosse* (Paris: Ch. Eggimann, 1911), pp. 86-90, 235-240; Garvan, *op. cit.*, pp. 6, 7; Drummond, *op. cit.*, p. 33. This building owes much to the earlier studies of Jacques Perret, published in *Des Fortifications et Artifices* (Paris, 1594).

[23] La Rochelle, built in 1603, designed by Philibert De l'Orme, seated 3,500; Dieppe, built in 1600, seated 6,000.

[24] On the destruction of the Huguenot temples, see the *Bulletin* of the Société de L'Histoire du Protestantisme Français, VIII (1859), 110; XXXIV (1885) 280-283.

In England, during that involved period of political and religious turmoil from 1527 when Henry VIII first determined to divorce Katherine of Aragon until the restoration of the Stuarts in 1660 following the Puritan ascendancy of the Protectorate, the various parties successively in power remodeled the churches to suit their own religious needs. Generally, communion tables were substituted for stone altars; and high pulpits, often richly carved, were introduced. Occasionally galleries were added to accommodate the growing congregations, and eventually box pews replaced the earlier benches.

The earliest English Protestant church of note, St. Paul's in Covent Garden, designed by Inigo Jones and built in 1640, is rectangular, with galleries along the two sides. In its basic elements—its simple shape, its clear sense of well-lit, enclosed, limited space, its galleries, and box pews—it not only embodied most of the characteristics of Protestant churches, but also anticipated the later work of Sir Christopher Wren, James Gibbs, and their American imitators.[25]

Wren was the creator of the Anglo-Saxon Protestant church, developed in his magnificent city churches built after the great fire of London in 1666. Wren built over 50 simple, restrained London churches which are characterized by their emphasis on a central preaching space. These churches, devoid of Christian symbolism but full of pagan and Erastian symbolism, were stylistically more responsive to a secular and international Palladianism than to any specific character of the English church.

The earliest Puritan places of worship in England were built after 1650, since the Puritans had the use of the old churches during the Protectorate. Their meeting places were designed as preaching houses, and were plain, often delicately plain. They typically had windows on three sides and a pulpit on the fourth, and since their basic aim

---

25Garvan, *op. cit.*, pp. 11-12.

was to provide as many seats as possible within view of the pulpit, they often had galleries on three sides. Sometimes a clear space was allowed in the middle for a communion table.[26]

Throughout Europe in the first two centuries after the Reformation, Protestant church architecture developed recognizable general characteristics dependent upon the new forms of worship, and expressive of that regained sense of the new community. In contrast to both earlier liturgical traditions and contemporary Catholic building, these new churches gathered their worshipers closely about a prominent pulpit in a clearly defined, well lighted space. And among some groups, notably the Dutch Reformed and the French Huguenot, ecclesiastical architecture was reduced to these bare requirements and transformed by them.

ARCHITECTURE IN THE NEW WORLD

European settlers brought with them to America the developed ideas of Protestant church architecture. Throughout the colonies, in spite of the differences caused by varying backgrounds and poor communication, the new churches were informed by the common Protestant characteristics evolved in Europe.

Most conservative and traditional in their expression of these were the Anglican churches in Virginia and Maryland. Indeed, St. Luke's Church in Isle of Wight County near Smithfield, Virginia, built in 1632, is a late example of a medieval tradition. A small brick building with buttressed walls, stepped gables, tracery windows, and entrance tower, it has been called "survival Gothic."[27] Others, such as Christ Church in Lancaster County, Virginia,

---

26John Betjeman, "Nonconformist Architecture," *Architectural Review*, LXXXVIII (December, 1940), 161-174, has described these buildings as an architecture for people who believed and argued, not for those who believed and sang, nor for those who believed and shouted. See M. S. Briggs, *Puritan Architecture* (London: Lutterworth Press, 1946).

27Andrew Landale Drummond, *Story of American Protestantism* (Boston: Beacon Press, 1950), pp. 12, 13.

built in 1732, show the quiet, intimate reverence of the
English country church, having shapely pulpits with
carved sounding boards, well proportioned altar pieces
with engraved Creed and Commandments, small transept
galleries with paneled fronts, box pews with armorial
bearings, barrel vaulted ceilings in plaster, and white
interiors. This tradition persisted in rural areas, and interesting variations in unpainted wood of these typical plaster interiors appear in Delaware in Prince George's Chap-
el near Dagsboro, built about 1757, and in Christ Church,
Broad Creek Hundred, near Laurel, built in 1770-1772.
Anglican churches in the metropolitan centers, notably
Christ Church in Philadelphia, designed by an amateur
architect, Dr. John Kearsley, and completed in 1754, are
typically in the English tradition established by Wren and
would not be out of place on a London street.

Early Lutheran churches in this country were built by
both German and Swedish settlers and are not only rec-
ognizably Protestant in their basic schemes, which gather
the congregations closely in a simple space about a high
pupit, but also reflect the countries of origin. The Swedes
built a church, which no longer exists, at Tinicum along
the Delaware River as early as 1646, but the two "Old
Swedes" churches, Gloria Dei in Philadelphia, dedicated
in 1700, and the slightly earlier Holy Trinity in Wilming-
ton, survive as monuments of the Swedish Lutheran settle-
ments on the Delaware, though both have been Episcopal
churches for many years.[28] Gloria Dei, built by the Rev.
Andrew Rudiman, a missionary sent by Charles XI of
Sweden, recalls contemporary Swedish architecture with
its compact shape and steep roofs. The original interior
appearance has been completely obscured by 1846 altera-

28John F. Watson, *Annals of Philadelphia and Pennsylvania in the Olden Time*, 2
vols., Vol. III by Willis P. Hazard (Philadelphia: E. S. Stuart, 1884), I, 39, 146-152,
III, 106-110. Also, drawings, photographs, and written data in the Historic American
Buildings Survey collections in the Library of Congress (hereafter HABS). See also
the standard source, Amandus Johnson, *The Swedish Settlement on the Delaware*,
2 vols. (Philadelphia: University of Pennsylvania, 1911).

tions,[29] but vestiges of the earlier Protestant plan are visible in the locations of the two main entrances, one under a tower at the west end and the other on the long south side.

Augustus Lutheran Church, built in 1743 for Dr. Heinrich Melchior Muhlenberg at Trappe, Pennsylvania, is perhaps the finest surviving example of the Lutheran variation on the early Protestant church.[30] It is a squat stone building with galleries on three sides and box pews closely grouped around a small altar and a high pulpit with sounding board. With simple architectural detail and ornament, it is like the small churches built in Germany after the Thirty Years' War, which have a domesticity not far removed from the homes of the peasants.[31] These churches seem ideally suited to a worship that is liturgical, but with a liturgy in which the people join. There is no frigid ecclesiasticism here where a black-robed pastor stands close to his congregation, but, rather, they express that communal sense found in the notion of the priesthood of all believers.

If the early Lutheran churches in this country patterned themselves after the architecture in the old countries, later ones were modeled after their neighbors, which were mostly English. The Rev. Nicholas Collin has left an account dated May 27, 1786, of problems involved in building a Lutheran church in a Swedish community on the New Jersey shore of the Delaware River in 1783-1784.[32] Pastor Collin wrote, ". . . it was necessary on every principle of prudence and public spirit to form the new church

29When the present floor, side galleries, pulpit, pews, and organ were installed.

30HABS. Writers' Program, *Pennsylvania, a Guide to the Keystone State* (New York: Oxford University Press, 1940), p. 429. *The Old Trappe Church, A Memorial of the Sesqui-Centennial Services of Augustus Evangelical Lutheran Church,* ed. Ernest T. Kretschmann (Philadelphia: Published by the Congregation, 1893), 60-70.

31The style of these churches was codified in a book issued to aid in the rebuilding after the war in 1649 by Joseph Furttenbach, the younger, *Kirchengebäude in was Form u. Gestalt nach gerecht erfordernder Mensur ein mittelgrosses . . . Kirchengebäulin . . . mit geringen Unkosten aufzubauen.*

32Federal Writers' Project, *The Record of the Swedish Lutheran Churches at Racoon and Penn's Neck 1713-1786,* introduction and notes by Amandus Johnson, published by the New Jersey Commission to Commemorate the 300th Anniversary of the Settlement by the Swedes and Finns on the Delaware (Elizabeth, New Jersey, 1938), pp. 184-187.

on a plan suitable to the prospect of a future age. Its dimensions ought to correspond with the increase of population for at least a century and its appearance with the gradual progress of taste in a country advancing fast to the modes of civilized life." Lutheran architecture in the New World, whether looking back to the old country in its early days or to the tastes of its alien neighbors in its later days, remained basically conservative.

Yet, under strong pietistic influences, American Lutheranism could revert to the extremely simple and austere forms of early Protestant architecture, as in the Hauge Norwegian Evangelical Lutheran Church near Daleyville, Wisconsin, built as late as 1852.[33] It is a square log structure, covered with clapboards, with a gallery around three sides centered, not on an altar, but on a high pulpit. Though only 22 feet square, it can seat well over a hundred people, and satisfies to an unusual degree that basic function of a Protestant church: to gather as many people as possible, through the simplest means, within hearing of the Word of God. The Protestant tradition of the high pulpit survived even among the state church adherents from Norway who settled at Muskego, Wisconsin, where they built their church with a high pulpit in 1845.

Quaker meeting houses have maintained a distinctive character over a long period, and a number of examples survive, especially in southeastern Pennsylvania.[34] They embody the Protestant ideal of plainness to an extreme degree, but the space of their simple interiors has no strong focus since Quaker worship has no place for preaching, and the churches do not have the characteristic high pulpits. The ideal of plainness, however, aspired to in all aspects of Quaker life and a controlling architectural principle, is strongly expressed in their meeting

---

[33]HABS.
[34]For an illustrated survey, with a short discussion of the bibliography, see Hubert Lidbetter, "Quaker Meeting Houses," *Architectural Review*, XCIX, No. 592 (April, 1946), 99-116. Also, John E. Eshelman, "Society of Friends and Their Meeting Houses in Berks County," *Berks County Historical Review*, I (1936), 34-40.

houses. In these simple structures, devoid of all ornament, yet built with an extraordinary and devoted craftsmanship and lighted by a clear, even light, the Quaker found an appropriate setting for his uniquely personal, spiritual religion.

In theocratic New England, where a particular notion of the Christian community was both a practical ethic and a motivating ideal, characteristics of the Protestant church type were combined and transformed into an artistic expression of the faith of the early Puritans.[35] The characteristic meeting house plan of these churches is nonliturgical in its arrangement, with galleries, box pews, and a movable communion table, and focuses on an elaborate pulpit, often with a sounding board. The interior space has a simple shape and is well lighted and clearly defined. The construction is not only simple but immediately apparent, and the limited ornament is abstract.

This meeting house plan obtained through most of the eighteenth century in New England. Though in the cities the gradual shift from meeting house to church began as early as 1723 in Christ Church (Old North) in Boston,[36] in the country the older tradition held on, and one of the finest surviving examples of the early type is the meeting house in Rockingham, Vermont, built as late as 1787.[37] Among the best known of these New England meeting houses is the very early one surviving in Hingham, Massachusetts, called the "Old Ship Meeting House," built in 1681.[38] It is characterized by a compact rectangular shape, a hip roof, and a principal entrance on the long

35Of the many works on New England meeting houses, see particularly: George Francis Marlowe, *Churches of Old New England* (New York: The Macmillan Company, 1947) ; Andrew Landale Drummond, "Evolution of the New England Meeting House," *Journal of the Royal Institute of British Architects*, June, 1946, pp. 337-342 ; Anthony N. B. Garvan, *Architecture and Town Planning in Colonial Connecticut* (New Haven, Conn.: Yale University Press, 1951) ; John F. Kelly, *Early Connecticut Meeting Houses* (New York: Columbia University Press, 1948).
36Marlowe, *op. cit.*, pp. 37-51.
37HABS. Herbert Wheaton Congdon, *Old Vermont Houses* (Brattleboro, Vt.: Stephen Daye Press, 1940).
38HABS. Marlowe, *op. cit.*, pp. 52-69. On the restoration of the building, see M. P. Corse in *Old Time New England* (published for the Society for the Preservation of New England Antiquities), July, 1930.

side rather than the end. The decorative character of the interior, which has an open trussed roof, is based upon a devoted attention to the necessary architectural detail.

In New England, where the franchise depended upon church membership, it was only natural that the meeting house should be not only a place of worship but also a hall of government. This theocratic idea underlay Puritan New England from the beginning. John Winthrop, in his sermon aboard the flagship Arabella, expressed it clearly when he said that life in the New World would be fulfilled "Under a due forme of Government both Civill and ecclesiasticall." The New England Puritan was not a lone pioneer on the frontier. The Puritans moved in groups, and their whole notion of their destiny was basically urban, even in the American wilderness. They felt called by God to establish his order on earth, and the town was their answer to this call.[39] The meeting house was the monument of the New England town, and in its lucid shelter, Puritan logic applied itself without discrimination to matters of theology and government.

AN EVALUATION

In architecture man creates an image of himself according to the way he understands himself in his world. It is inescapable. If he builds in a commensurate form, with the various parts in refined relationship, self-aware, assertive, against the landscape, he is recognizable as a Greek from the fifth century before Christ; if he builds in an incommensurate form, enclosing heaven on earth in a glittering sheath, never fully revealed, and clothes himself in ceremonial panoply, he is recognizable as a sixth century Constantinopolitan; if he builds a tense and incomprehensible form, enclosing a processional space, barely visible in a dark-colored light, he is recognizable as a twelfth century

---

[39]Perry Miller, *Errand Into the Wilderness* (Cambridge, Mass.: Belknap Press of Harvard University Press, 1956), Chapters I, V.

Frenchman; even if he chooses to imitate the forms built by his heroes from the past, he is not confused with those heroes but is recognizable by his profoundly nostalgic romanticism as a recent American. This basic architectural fact holds true for individuals: the world of forms man creates about him, or even the fact that out of insensitivity or willfulness he may ignore the forms about him, reveals in a ruthlessly accurate way, devoid of apology, without literary aggrandizement, more pertinently than he could say it, his view of himself in relation to his world —and where individuals constitute a community, the artistic expression of that community reveals a world in which particular individuals have found their identity.

After the fifteenth century, Western man, whether Catholic or Protestant, no longer saw himself in a Gothic world. The Catholic in Italy, Spain, or Middle America, freed from his old world by the Renaissance, was caught up in the contrapuntal movement of a baroque world, richly illusionistic, hierarchically organized, of this world, yet full of miracles and saints.

In contrast to the forms of both earlier eras and contemporary Catholic culture, the architecture of the early Protestants in general was neither processional, nor hierarchical, nor illusionistic, nor meditative, nor mystical, nor contemplative. The Protestant found his identity in a close congregation within a clear space, surrounded by forms accountable by human logic. Except in the churches of those sects, like the Quakers, where a unique, individualistic inner spirit was at the heart of their belief, the focal point of the early Protestant churches was the high pulpit, that one piece of furniture, usually in an appropriately exalted form, essential to expounding the Word of God.

Early Protestant churches in general satisfy Calvin's first requirement of ecclesiastical architecture, that it functionally satisfy the new forms of worship. On this level, that Protestant sense of community seen in a common

emphasis on preaching spaces and clear, simple shapes iden-
tifies these churches as a group. It is on the level of Calvin's
second requirement, that these practical functions unique
to Protestant worship be artistically transformed and unified as an expression of the faith, where differences appear.

Troeltsch's distinction between the social conservatism
of the church-type of Protestantism and the social liberalism of the sect-type is useful for explaining the different
tendencies that appear in Protestant architecture.[40] The
socially conservative church-type felt less called to answer
Calvin's second requirement than the sect-type. This does
not mean that the Lutheran and Anglican churches are
architecturally inferior—it would be absurd to argue that
Wren's London city churches or their great influence is
bad. It does mean that the architecture of these conservative Protestant groups was more affected by local customs
or international developments in art having nothing to do
with religion, and it does indicate that the basic religious
concerns of these groups were, in practical ways, not so
strongly related to this world.

There is no simple Lutheran spirit in church architecture. Lutheranism was not a social force in the same way
Puritanism, for example, was, and part of its genius is
that it can minister to different kinds of people under
varying situations. Since Lutheranism did not create a
society of its own, its churches could reflect such divergent
worlds as that of the Norwegian frontiersman of the
American Midwest, or of the cosmopolitan Dresdener in
an international art center.

The sect-type of Protestantism, which profoundly affected a wide range of social forms, more nearly answered
Calvin's second requirement of ecclesiastical architecture.
Of the various aspects of Protestantism, it is the worldly
asceticism of Calvinism that seems to have been most

40Troeltsch, *op. cit.*, particularly II, 561-578.

clearly expressed in architecture.[41] The Puritans might eliminate the other arts from their lives, but they could not avoid architecture. They could only strip it of all its extra attractions, and their aesthetic expression was limited to form. They created structures that were simple and direct, spaces that were well lighted and clearly limited, schemes that were directly functional. Through a refinement of proportion and the articulation resulting from careful craftsmanship, their buildings were artistically unified as expressions of these severe ideals. Their churches may be austere, but they only reflect a view of the world based upon a religion that was ascetic. Part of the appeal of these simple churches, which would be difficult to overestimate even today, may lie in the fact that Puritanism is more than a historical religious movement. The ascetism of Puritanism is a continuing aspect of Protestantism that criticizes and purifies established social forms. In Puritan New England, where this worldly asceticism reached its fullest social development, one can most properly speak of a Protestant style in architecture.

41Max Weber, *The Protestant Ethic and the Spirit of Capitalism*, translated by Talcott Parsons (New York: Charles Scribner's Sons, 1958), discusses most clearly the extent to which this worldly asceticism underlies modern Western history.